FLORENCE ✦ EXPLORED

FLORENCE ✦ EXPLORED

RUPERT SCOTT

NEW AMSTERDAM
New York

For Julian

Library of Congress Cataloging
in Publication Data
Scott, Rupert
ISBN 0–941533–15–8 (cloth)
ISBN 0–941533–16–6 (paper)
© Rupert Scott 1987
First American edition published in 1988
by New Amsterdam Books,
by arrangement with The Bodley Head Ltd., London.

NEW AMSTERDAM BOOKS
171 Madison Avenue
New York, NY 10016

CONTENTS

Introduction, 13

1. Piazza del Duomo to Or San Michele, 25
2. The Piazza and Palazzo della Signoria, 45
3. The Bargello and S. Croce, 59
4. The Uffizi, 87
5. The Medici, S. Lorenzo and S. Marco, 105
6. The Oltrarno, 123
7. Florence of the Grand Dukes: The Palazzo Pitti, 149
8. S. Maria Novella to Ognissanti, 175
9. SS. Annunziata, the Accademia and S. Maria Maddalena dei Pazzi, 195
10. The Florentine Environs, 213

Appendix I. Places of interest not mentioned in the text or not normally open to the public, and some Medici villas, 221

Appendix II. Opening times, 227

Index, 233

ACKNOWLEDGEMENTS

Many thanks to Dottoressa Meloni and other staff at the Soprintendenza delle Belle Arti, to Hugh Honour, John Fleming and Charles McCorquodale for reading the type-script, to Sir Harold Acton for many useful suggestions, my Father for his generosity and unfailing encouragement, to Susan Smith for her photographic research, to Richard Fremantle for the use of his tower, to The Bodley Head, Simon Wells, Dieter Klein, the Kunsthistorisches Institut in Florence, the Librarian of the British Institute and the management of the Pensione Bandini.

LIST OF ILLUSTRATIONS

To key the photographs to the text the relevant number is printed in the text in bold type at the appropriate place.

1. Panorama of Florence, 18th-century engraving by Valerio Spada, x–xi
2. English tourists admire 'il bel cielo d'Italia', cartoon by *C. Teja* in Pasquino, 21
3. Florence from the hill of S. Miniato, painting by J. M. Turner, 1818, 23
4. The façade of the Duomo, a 19th-century photograph, 30
5. The façade of the Duomo, a 14th-century drawing, 31
6. The cupola of the Duomo, an engraving by G. B. Nelli, 1753, 33
7, 8. The Mercato Vecchio, 19th-century photographs, 36–7
9. Piazza della Signoria in the 18th century, painting by Bernardo Bellotto, 43
10. Cosimo I, painting by Agnolo Bronzino, 51
10a. The Loggia dei Lanzi, 56
11. Francesco I as a child, painting by Agnolo Bronzino, 52

12. The Badia and Bargello, 18th-century engraving by Giuseppe Zocchi, 60
13. The courtyard of the Bargello in 1786, as the torture implements are burned, 62
14. Portrait of Dante in the Bargello, 68
15. S. Croce, the façade before completion, 19th-century photograph, 75
16. Piazza S. Croce (during 1966 flood) with the statue of Dante, 76
17. S. Croce cloister during flood of 1966, 84
18. The Uffizi seen from the riverside, 18th-century engraving by Giuseppe Zocchi, 89
19. The Tribuna, 18th-century painting by Johann Zoffany, 99
20. S. Lorenzo, the façade and piazza, early photograph, 109
21. The Mercato Centrale, photograph, 117
22. Piazza S. Trinita, early photograph, 124
23. Lungarno Corsini from south of the river, 18th-century engraving by Giuseppe Zocchi, 128

24. S. Spirito, projected façade designed in the 1830s, 134
25. The Via Guicciardini approach to Ponte Vecchio demolished during the war, 136
26. The Ponte Vecchio from the Ponte alle Grazie, pre-war photograph, 138
27. The Ponte alle Grazie with the Arno in flood, 19th-century engraving, 143
28. Wool-dyeing factories on Lungarno Diaz, early photograph, 144
29. The Pitti Palace in the 16th century, with the Boboli Gardens and Belvedere, painting by Gustave Utens, 150
30. The Pitti Palace as extended, 18th-century engraving by Cosimo Mogalli, 152
31. Anna Maria, the Electress Palatine, portrait by Antonio Franchi, 153
32. Gian Gastone, portrait by Richter, 155
33, 34. Ferdinando II and Vittoria della Rovere, portraits by Jan Sustermans, 156–7
35. Elisa Bacciochi, portrait by Pietro Benvenuti, 162
36. Pietro Leopoldo and his family, portrait by J. A. U. Moll, 167
37. Piazza S. Maria Novella, 18th-century engraving, 184
38. Palazzo Strozzi, early photograph, 186
39. Piazza SS. Annunziata, 18th-century engraving by Giuseppe Zocchi, 197
40. Piazza S. Pier Maggiore, 18th-century engraving by Giuseppe Zocchi, 209
41. Florence from Bellosguardo, 19th-century painting by John Brett, 219
42. Medici villa at Poggio a Caiano, painting by Gustave Utens, 224

Grateful acknowledgements to the following Collections for permission to reproduce the illustrations in this volume:

Gabinetto fotografico, Soprintendenza beni artistici e storici, Florence, for Nos 1, 4, 10–15, 23, 26, 28–34, 36, 37, 39, 40 and 42; Italfotogieffe, Florence, for Nos 6–8, 16, 17, 20, 22, 25, 27 and 38; a private collection for No. 3; Museo dell' Opera del Duomo, Florence, for No. 5; the Szepmuveszeti Museum, Budapest, for No. 9; Barnaby's Picture Library, for No. 10a; the Collection of Her Majesty the Queen (copyright reserved) for No. 19; the Conway Library, Courtauld Institute of Art, London, for No. 21; the Convent of S. Spirito, Florence, for No. 24; Museo Stibbert, Florence, for No. 35; and the Tate Gallery, London, for No. 41.

LIST OF MAPS AND PLANS

1. Piazza del Duomo to Or San Michele, 24
2. Piazza della Signoria, 44
3. The Bargello and S. Croce, 58
4. Plan of S. Croce, 78
5. The Medici, S. Lorenzo and S. Marco, 104
6. The Oltrarno (West), 122
7. The Oltrarno (East), 140
8. S. Maria Novella to Ognissanti, 174
9. Plan of S. Maria Novella, 178
10. SS. Annunziata, the Accademia and S. Ambrogio, 194

(Drawn by Simon Wells and the author)

1. Panorama of Florence, 18th-century engraving by Valerio Spada.

INTRODUCTION

✤ 'For every traveller who has any taste of his own,' wrote Aldous Huxley, 'the only useful guide book will be the one that he himself has written. All others are an exasperation. They mark with asterisks the works of art which he finds dull, and they pass over in silence those which he admires. They make him travel long miles to see a pile of rubbish; they go into ecstasies over mere antiquity . . . In a word they are intolerable.' I tremble to think of the words that he might have found to condemn *Florence Explored* which, as a guide book to what he once described as 'a second-rate provincial town' full of '. . . repulsive Gothic architecture and acres of Christmas-card primi-

tives . . . colonised by English sodomites and middle-aged lesbians', could be described as a combination of the two evils. I fear he might have said something in the same vein because like that brilliant and amusing, wonderfully sybaritic and in every way admirable minor classic *Venice for Pleasure* by J. G. Links which is its inspiration and which it in a limited way attempts to emulate, this little book is both eccentrically and arbitrarily selective. I have tried hard not to ask the reader to walk long miles to see piles of rubbish, not to gush over mere antiquity or to mark with asterisks works which you will find dull, but if like Huxley you prefer comprehensive guide books in the

Baedeker mould you will not enjoy *Florence Explored*. For this is a personal guide to the pleasures and the beauties of Florence, and our conception of pleasure and beauty may not be the same.

It would, however, be a mistake to think that this book bears any more than a passing resemblance to *Venice for Pleasure*. Florence is not perfectly suited, unlike Venice, to a guide that is largely topographical. Florence is and always has been a city that gives most pleasure to those who take their pleasures seriously. The single most compelling reason for coming here is to see Florentine Art. Thus it is in galleries and churches that users of this guide will spend the greater part of their days. Since Florence has possibly a denser concentration of beautiful works of art than any other city in the world, this can hardly be seen as an insupportable burden.

This, of course, is not to decry the austere but undeniable beauty of central Florence which offers the visitor abundant pleasures. The square mile or so that contains the *centro storico* is of a unique diversity. The shortest walk—from S. Spirito to S. Trinita, for instance, or from SS. Annunziata to Piazza della Signoria—is an odyssey that leads from streets where delicious smells of syrupy resin waft from artisans' workshops, past markets piled with vegetables and game, down streets crowded with students and into grand baroque axes flanked by palazzi as formidable as the Florentine nobility that own them. And all this time the experience is enlivened and the walker tantalised by chance views of the Duomo or the Arno, by the endless contrast between buildings of different scales and centuries and, above all, by the Florentines themselves. Impeccably dressed in Botticelli reds, Pontormo greens and Bronzino blues, looking at tourists with all the *hauteur* we might expect from the heirs of Cellini and Vasari, they are the greatest of all the 'sights', though it may sound patronising to say so. Despite decades of mass tourism Florentine street life remains miraculously vivacious and it is this, as much as its art and its buildings, that is the city's charm. That it is necessary to have reactions faster than those of an electric eel to avoid Vespas going the wrong way down one-way streets, or cars shooting the red lights and driving along the pavement; that it is often difficult to hear yourself think, let alone talk, for the noise seems a small price to pay for the pleasure of being a spectator in a place where everyone seems twice as alive as anywhere else.

* * *

Nothing is more boring at the beginning of a guide book than a thick 'historical introduction'. One immediately flicks through to its last page and makes a note to read it on the flight home. But, having said that, I am going to begin with a little Florentine history, for nothing will enhance your visit more than an idea, however sketchy, of the city's past. It effectively begins, as with so many other cities in Europe, with the Romans. Florence was a typical medium-sized, reasonably prosperous town-cum-military camp. It had a large amphitheatre, temples, a small forum and market place and a bridge somewhere near the present site of the Ponte Vecchio. Of all this quite amazingly little survives. Roman Florence was destroyed during the long painful collapse of the western Empire and the centuries of Dark Ages that followed. Florence was sacked by invading hordes of Goths, Lombards and then by the rather less barbaric Franks under Charlemagne. It was then gradually effaced by its own citizens who used their ruins as a convenient quarry for building stone.

Apart from the occasional and not particularly helpful glimmer of information — like the date of a saint's execution or the foundation of a long since vanished church — nothing is really known about Florence from Roman times until the eleventh century when, like other cities in Tuscany, it began a slow recovery and rise to prosperity by exploiting its position of strategic importance in the wars between Pope and Emperor for control of the Italian peninsula. The Florentines, showing an early capacity for backing the right horse, sided with the eventual victors — the Papacy — while managing to extract the maximum number of concessions from both sides. The first signs of this recovery are some of the most beautiful buildings in Italy — the Tuscan Romanesque churches of which the most important are the Baptistery and S. Miniato — with green and white façades of a surprisingly 'clean' classical derivation that are unique to Florence and quite unlike the contemporary buildings erected by her neighbouring city states.

All Florentine historians are unashamedly partisan, but none more so than Giovanni Villani, who conceived a plan to write his *History of the Florentine People* of 1334 after a Gibbon-like inspiration on the Roman Capitol a decade earlier. According this lively if highly unreliable source, by the second quarter of the fourteenth century Florence had a population of some 90,000 people, though this statistic has to be treated with some suspicion as he arrives at it through the unusually unscientific method of calculating the amount of food entering the city and working backwards to arrive at a figure. But it cannot, unfortunately, be checked since the population was officially recorded by the equally unscientific method of dropping beads into a vase at the centre of the Baptistery every time a child was born. But even when allowances are made for exaggeration, the extent of the Florentine economic miracle is indeed amazing, and can never be really plausibly explained. Without large areas of fertile agricultural plain to exploit and without convenient access to the sea Florence had now become one of the largest manufacturing centres in Europe and perhaps the richest city in Italy.

Few fields of historical study, however, can be much more depressing than later medieval Florence. It is dominated by the infamous, endless and inpenetrably complex wars between the Guelphs, who were nominally the supporters of the Papacy and the Ghibellines, who backed the Holy Roman Empire. It may seem remarkable but it is possible to read one of the many books written about these wars and to reach the last page having understood little more than one had on the first about the causes of their feuds. It is simplest to leave Florentine history until the opening years of the fifteenth century by which time, after a great many small wars with her neighbours, after endless advances, retreats, defeats and victories and with a mixture of good fortune, skill, and courage the Florentines controlled an area that stretched from the Mediterranean to the Marches. Though Lucca was never a part of the contado, and Siena remained independent until the 1550s, Florence was clearly the capital of Tuscany by 1400. Florence was governed by its merchant élite—the two or three hundred families who controlled the economic life of the city through banking, manufacturing and commerce. By dominating a system of government based on corruptly elected committees they managed to manipulate the city in their own interests. It was, to a large extent, the patronage provided by these families to the pool of artists and craftsmen employed by Florentine industry that created the explosion of creative talent called the early Renaissance. And it was from this class that a family emerged to dominate the history of Florence for over three hundred years—the Medici.

Medici rule in Florence divides itself into two broad and distinct phases. In the first, which lasts from 1434 to 1494, though living in a palazzo fit for a Prince and in possession of a fortune rather larger than that of any other Florentine family, they were merely private citizens, and have sometimes been compared to the mafia leaders of New York or Chicago during the twenties and thirties. The comparison works surprisingly well: Cosimo 'il Vecchio', the political founder of the dynasty often seems, if you read his letters, rather like Don Corleone in *The Godfather*—discreetly ruthless, conspicuously generous when in the public eye, politically adept and guided above all by an intense family loyalty. He carefully destroyed the power of his enemies and opponents, while gradually increasing the influence of the Medici over domestic and foreign politics. An indication of his success is the ease with which his son and grandson assumed his unofficial position as *éminence grise* to the Republic.

The cliché that one generation makes a fortune, the next uses it and the third generation spends it is peculiarly apt of the early Medici. The fortune was made, principally by financing the papal Curia, by Giovanni di Averardo de' Medici (1360–1429). His son Cosimo 'il Vecchio' was more ambitious and used the fortune to build up influence and take power. His great-grandson Lorenzo 'the Magnificent' was largely responsible for its dispersal. He ignored the activities of the Medici bank to such an extent that it had virtually ceased to function at his death in 1492. During the last years of his life he was in serious financial difficulties, being forced to 'borrow', meaning take, from state funds more than once to cover his and the bank's debts. His fame rests not on his achievements as a businessman but as a politician, diplomat and patron of the arts, particularly of literature.

If it was money that brought the Medici into power then it was a shortage of it that greatly contributed to their fall. A combination of declining prestige and the incompetence of Lorenzo's children forced the Medici into a lonely exile from 1494 to 1507. However unhappy their fate during these years, it was less painful than that suffered by their immediate successor in Florence, a fanatical Dominican friar called Fra Girolamo Savonarola who was burnt at the stake in the Piazza della Signoria.

The Medici might never have been heard of again had it not been for the extremely successful ecclesiastical career of Lorenzo's son Giovanni. Created a Cardinal aged 16, he rose, despite alarming signs of laziness in youth, to be one of the great Renaissance Popes, Leo X. Following established sixteenth-century Papal convention, he used the still massive influence of his office for what the Medici saw as its natural purpose—the political advancement of his own family. The Medici were restored to Florence and his nephew Giulio became Pope Clement VII. Expelled once again by the ungrateful Florentines in 1527, they were restored once more in 1530, this time with an Imperial title, in the unprepossessing form of Alessandro de' Medici. Perhaps not the most tactful of rulers, Alessandro managed to offend his not entirely favourably disposed subjects in many ways, but particularly badly by publicly smashing the Florentine 'liberty bell' from the tower of the Piazza della Signoria. He managed, however, to last seven years and to build the Fortezza da Basso before being murdered by his equally unpleasant first cousin Lorenzaccio. The assassin's knife does much to clear the air. The fog of complication now lifts over the history of Florence and the second phase of Medici domination effectively begins.

Murder, war and ecclesiastical careers had by now left the Medici so thin on the ground that it was necessary, in effect, to invent one. The Florentine authorities were forced to turn to a distant 18-year-old cousin of Alessandro called Cosimo de' Medici who, against the expectations of all, turned out to be a natural statesman, firmly establishing his own position and laying the foundations of a dynasty that was to survive for two hundred years until the death in 1737 of the last Grand Duke Gian Gastone I.

Though at least one among Cosimo's heirs, Ferdinando I (ruled, 1587–1609), took a dedicated interest in the affairs of the state, they were, rather like the French Bourbons in the eighteenth century, bored by politics and, happily for visitors to Florence today, sought diversion in the arts. They lived in an atmosphere of stiff magnificence that impressed even those from larger and richer countries. In the state rooms of the Palazzo Pitti they wallowed amongst paintings of their ancestors, furniture in jade and silver, portraits by Raphael and Titian and endless court intrigue. Considering the indulgence of their lives and their ability to choose indescribably unattractive and bad-tempered wives, it is surprising that they

managed to remain sane for so long but, as it was, their end was painfully protracted. Cosimo III, a pious old bore, reigned for fifty-one tedious years until his death in 1723. As his enlightened elder son Prince Ferdinando was by this stage already dead, the throne passed to the dissolute Gian Gastone, who reigned for fourteen not very happy years, mostly spent, acording to *The Last Medici* by Sir Harold Acton, lying in bed surrounded by a crowd of hangers-on who amused him in various bizarre ways. His more staid but no less unhappy sister, Anna Maria the Electress Palatine, died four years later, and in the most important and generous gesture of Medicean history, left the entire family collections to the citizens of Florence.

With the death of Gian Gastone Tuscany passed, after a complex eighteenth-century game of dynastic musical chairs, to the Dukes of Lorraine and became (through their marriage to Maria Theresa) an independent state within the Habsburg dominions. After a bad start, melting down the Medici jewels, ransacking the treasury and even worse, cancelling the Medicean Holidays, they turned out to be the kindliest, most paternal-istic men and some of the most intelligent rul-ers in Europe. Maria Theresa's son Pietro Leo-poldo acceded to the Grand Duchy in 1765 and from then until his death in the 1790s established a reputation as Europe's most enlightened despot, reducing taxes, draining marshes and encouraging landowners to build thousands and thousands of the simple stone *case coloniche* now considered so desirable.

Ferdinand III, Leopold's son, spent the duration of the Napoleonic wars in Salzburg, while Tuscany was ruled first by a faintly absurd King of Etruria, then from 1809 to 1814 by Napoleon's sister Elisa Bacciochi-Bonaparte. In 1815 they returned to preside over some of the happiest decades in Florentine history, from 1815 to 1859. If it were possible to be reincarnated, one would find few other epochs in modern civilisation pro-ffering more temptations. An earthly paradise continually at peace and ruled by a benevolent prince, without railways, with an almost uncen-sored press, weekly balls at the Palazzo Pitti and a buoyant intellectual life, Florence quickly became

a haven for foreign residents. (2) Prices were absurdly cheap—houses could be rented for next to nothing and wine was given away free in a plentiful *vendemmia*. Grass grew in the streets, the gates of the city were still locked every day at dusk, as they had been since the thirteenth cen-tury. Florence, delightfully isolated from the rest of the world, was still the centre of an economy that was entirely agricultural—in fact one of the largest industries in Tuscany until 1860 was a factory in Prato making straw hats.

The earthly paradise had to endure many changes in the years that followed. The last Grand Duke, Leopold III, was strangely bewildered by his subjects' desire for change when everything seemed so perfectly agreeable, but declared him-self in favour of a united Italy and honourably abdicated in the autumn of 1859.

Florence, governed from Turin for six years, itself became the capital of Italy in 1865–70. Although this was to bring unquestioned econ-omic benefits, in some respects its price was very high. A city that had remained virtually untouched since the sixteenth century, with large

2 Cartoon from *Pasquino* of English tourists looking at 'Il bel cielo d'Italia'

tracts of open countryside within its walls and orchards beyond them, was now exposed to the tender mercies of a government that was uncompromising in its efforts to achieve 'progress' and efface all memories of the recent past. The transfer of the capital to Florence caused an immediate influx of as many as thirty thousand new residents, who were largely accommodated in unattractive new suburbs beyond the city walls, which were demolished for no good reason in 1865. In the late 1880s the most interesting part of Florence, the ghetto, was destroyed to make way for the eminently forgettable Piazza della Repubblica. Ironically, it was while Florence endured this treatment that it enjoyed an artistic and intellectual Indian summer, becoming the centre of Italian impressionism, a great social centre and the home of celebrated writers and scholars such as Bernard Berenson and Gabriele d'Annunzio.

Though untouched by the First World War, Florence suffered badly in the Second. It is ironic that one of Hitler's few recorded acts of cultural clemency—a personal order that the Ponte Vecchio, which he had seen and admired in 1938, be spared—should have resulted in a much worse loss, the destruction of the borghi at its either end, which were mined in order to block its access roads. Appalling disaster though this was, permanently scarring the core of the city, and transforming its most beautiful streets into its worst eyesores, Florence was fortunate not to be damaged more badly, and has been just as fortunate since then in having a local government that has rebuilt the Ponte S. Trinita as a perfect facsimile and preserved most of the wonderful country immediately to the south from speculative building. The contado still sweeps right up to the walls of Forte del Belvedere and S. Miniato, which permits the delectable and rare sensation of being able to move in a single step from the city gates to the country, as if in a medieval town (3). But enough history, the time has arrived to see for yourself.

3

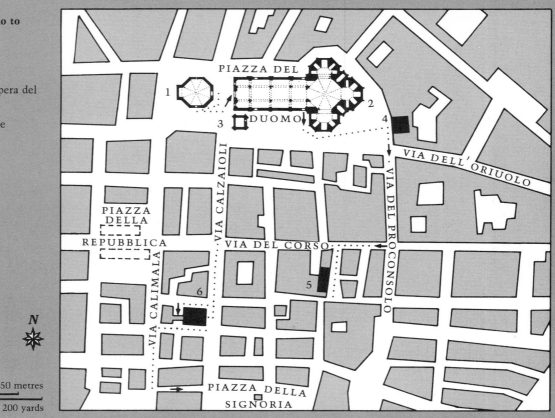

Map 1
Piazza del Duomo to
Or San Michele

1. Baptistery
2. Duomo
3. Campanile
4. Museo dell' Opera del Duomo
5. Casa di Dante
6. Or San Michele

PIAZZA DEL

DUOMO

VIA DELL' ORIUOLO

VIA CALZAIOLI

VIA DEL PROCONSOLO

PIAZZA DELLA

REPUBBLICA

VIA DEL CORSO

VIA CALIMALA

PIAZZA DELLA

SIGNORIA

N

0   50   100   150 metres

200 yards

1

PIAZZA DEL DUOMO
—*to*—
OR SAN MICHELE

✤ The Piazza del Duomo, we must admit, is not the most inviting or atmospheric place to begin a guide to Florence. It is a touch on the noisy side, often a little crowded and is hardly a place to linger in cafés admiring the view, even if there were any cafés in which to linger. But all this must be taken in good part, for the **Baptistery**, the octagonal building at the centre of the Piazza, is the best place to begin any exploration of the city. Both within and without it represents the first blossoming of Florentine art and provides a connection with the earliest days of the city's history. It was built sometime between the fifth and the eighth centuries A.D., largely from the stones and col-umns of the original Roman colony of Florentia, thought (on no very firm ground) to have been established in 72 B.C. by Caesar. Its solemn and impressive interior, ringed by granite columns matched to an assortment of different capitals, casts you back in an instant to the 'Dark Ages'— the centuries following the fall of the Roman Empire when for the early Christians their faith, of which a church like this was both symbol and guardian, can have been just about the only diver-sion from an existence overshadowed by danger and hardship and the Baptistery played a role in most aspects of Florentine life. Like S. Marco in Venice, the Baptistery had twin functions—

secular and ecclesiastical—in medieval Florence. It was here that the Florentines would bless soldiers before a battle or say prayers to avert the plague and, of course, baptise their children. The population was recorded by dropping beads into a large vase that stood at the centre of the church, a black bead for a boy and a white bead for a girl, which, though an adequate and attractive system in its own way, must be blamed for the dearth of reliable figures for the population of Florence before 1400.

The earliest surviving decoration is the tessellated section of the floor immediately to our right as we enter, which dates from the mid-twelfth century and represents signs of the Zodiac. The mosaic ceiling (late thirteenth to early fourteenth century), the finest example of the art in the West outside Venice and Ravenna and the last great triumph of the Byzantine style outside those two cities, is one of those works of art that perfectly expresses the values of the age in which it was created. A vast and menacing figure of *Christ*, 28 feet tall, stands in judgement over his flock. To one side of him are the Saved, enjoying the com-

forts of heaven, to the other are the Damned, enduring the sort of tortures that Dante took such pleasure in describing in the *Inferno*. The four bands of mosaic on the opposite side of the ceiling depict (top band) the *Creation of the World* and the stories of Joseph, Christ and John the Baptist; they are equally ferocious.

Early Renaissance art is represented by the superb tomb of John XXIII (not the amiable bespectacled Pope who instituted the Second Vatican Council but an unfortunate fifteenth-century antipope recognised by no-one except the Florentines) by Donatello and Michelozzo. The tomb is placed between two columns—an arrangement that is made to appear less uncomfortable than it might by the subtle visual device of enclosing the bay with half drawn drapes. In contrast with the ceiling it reflects a spiritual self-confidence typical of the Renaissance. Lying on the softest of cushions, with the Madonna above him and three angels below, John XXIII seems already well on the way to the luxuries of a papal heaven.

The fame of the Baptistery rests, however, not on its interior, impressive though it is, but on its three pairs of bronze doors. Perhaps the least interesting are those on the southern (entrance) side which are the earliest and were made between 1300 and 1330 by Andrea Pisano. It is interesting to look first at his simple and still clearly Gothic narrative scenes (the upper twenty depict the *Life of St John the Baptist* and the lower eight the *Theological Virtues*) with gilded figures set in relief within repeating quatrefoil frames; then to walk round to the north (opposite) side of the Baptistery where there is another, at first sight rather similar, pair of gates of a century later. These were begun in 1402 and made by Lorenzo Ghiberti (1378–1455), an important figure in the early Renaissance who wrote his own history of art and a wonderfully conceited autobiography from which he emerges as the first Florentine artist of memorable personality.

In a famous competition, thought to be the first authenticated public contest of its kind in the history of art, Ghiberti won the commission at the expense of the favourite, Filippo Brunelleschi (their trial panels of the *Sacrifice of Isaac* are now in the Bargello) then more famous as a sculptor than as an architect. While maintaining Pisano's basic scheme of 28 quatrefoiled panels, Ghiberti's doors make many innovations. The scenes are more complex, they have greater depth, are more dramatic and more lively than those by Pisano. A change in his style can be observed over the twenty-odd years that it took to make them. He moves from the traditional *Annunciation* (left door, third row from the top) composed around a prophet clad in long, swinging robes to the *Flagellation of Christ* (right door, second row from top) whose almost naked body stands before a classical arcade.

Ghiberti's name might, none the less, mean little to us today had he not been commissioned to make a second pair of bronze doors that now face the Cathedral on the eastern side of the Baptistery. Started in 1424 they were not hung until a few months before his death in 1455. It is with these second doors that he moves from inspired competence to genius. He entirely alters the overall design, reducing the number of panels from the original 28 to 10, dispensing with the original Gothic quatrefoils and making the panels much larger and the scenes more complex. More intricately worked, filled with shouting, seething groups of figures, with distant landscapes covered in pines and cypresses and grand classical buildings, they are expressive in a way that his first doors are not. Michelangelo, in the most enduring of his one-liners called them 'worthy to be the gates of paradise'.

His most important innovation was to vary the depth of relief on the panels to suggest a sense of recession and to achieve the same effect of perspective that fascinated painters. This is done with the utmost subtlety and technical expertise, as you can see by looking at any one of the panels, but in particular at *Jacob and Esau* (middle row, left) in which the architecture recedes into the infinite distance, though the panel itself has a virtually unbroken surface unity. The transformation of Ghiberti's style between one set of doors and the other is so dramatic that many assume that these were designed with the advice of Donatello, the greatest and most innovative sculptor of the fifteenth century.

The Baptistery's fine façades seem even more impressive if put in their historical context. They date from the twelfth and thirteenth centuries and are considered to be the first example of an original Florentine style in architectural decoration. They draw their inspiration not from the Romanesque buildings of central Italy built in the preceding centuries but directly from the architecture of ancient Rome. The simple, geometric design of the inlaid marble coordinates with the building's structure and bears little resemblance to the façades of contemporary churches built by Florence's neighbours, Lucca and Pisa, which are embellished with repeating tiers of dwarf arcades.

*　　*　　*

Detached from the Cathedral stands the **Campanile di Giotto**. It was much admired by Ruskin to whom it seemed the perfect combination of craft and sophistication. He called it the 'model and mirror of perfect architecture . . . a serene height of mountain alabaster coloured like a morning cloud and chased like a sea shell'. Henry James, rather pretentiously, went one step further. The Campanile was the finest achievement of a culture in which, he said '. . . the abiding felicity, the sense of saving sanity, of something sound and human predominates, offering a medium still conceivable for life.' Certainly it has a quality of unobtrusive, restrained but confident 'good taste' that is peculiarly Florentine. It took a very long time to build. Though named after Giotto, at his death in 1337 it had only reached a height of twelve feet, and if his succeeding architect, Andrea Pisano, had not doubled the thickness of its walls it would certainly have fallen down. Giotto, however, designed many of the plaques set into the façade (now replaced by replicas) describing the *Spiritual Progress of Man* through the arts, labour and the sacraments. These were also much admired by Ruskin, who devoted several eloquent, and by Ruskinian standards wonderfully brief, paragraphs of his guide book *Mornings in Florence* to them: 'Read but once these jewels,' he says, 'and your hour's study will give you strength for life.' The sculptures above them are replicas of figures by Donatello now in the Museo dell' Opera del Duomo.

If we feel energetic we might now climb the 414 steps to the top of the Campanile which the old *Baedeker* describes as 'a gentle and easy climb', though that is not my own experience. If we feel less energetic we might look at the lavish and now no longer universally admired neo-Gothic façade of the Cathedral, or **Duomo**, which contrasts uncomfortably with the restrained Baptistery which it faces. It was built between 1875 and 1886 at an enormous cost met largely from donations by the numerous community of foreign residents in Florence (some of whose names are recorded in diamond-shaped plaques at eye level) and unveiled in the presence of Queen Victoria, the Prime Minister of Italy and others. Photographs 4 and 5 (overleaf) show us earlier façades. That in Photograph 5 was begun in the fourteenth century but was never finished and eventually pulled down in 1587–8 to make way for a grand new classical façade that was never built. For the next three centuries it was left as in Photograph 4.

Those who have experienced the soaring splendour of French Gothic sometimes feel a little disappointed by the chilly and sparse decoration of the Duomo's interior, though at the same time they are usually astounded at the sheer bulk and

strength of its columns and vaults and by the size of the spaces they enclose. That, of course, is its intended effect—its beauty is its bulk, and the walls of the nave have been deliberately kept free of monuments, tombs or any other visual distractions to the soaring power of the structure.

When, at the end of the thirteenth century, the Florentines tore down the existing and inadequately grand Cathedral of S. Reparata, which then occupied this site, they had no doubt about the sort of building they wanted in its place. A pompous edict of 1296 announced that 'an edifice will be constructed so magnificent in its height and beauty that it will surpass anything of its kind built by the Greeks and the Romans.' The plans for the new Cathedral were twice enlarged during the course of the fourteenth century, unlike in Siena where the ravages caused by war and plague forced the city to leave the vast Duomo Nuovo incomplete and unroofed. Until the Papacy embarked on its own and even more terrifyingly ambitious scheme for the rebuilding of St Peter's in the sixteenth century it was the largest church in Western Christendom.

Among the few embellishments in the nave are the pair of equestrian paintings of famous *condottieri* by Paolo Uccello and Andrea del Castagno, the two most talented painters active in Florence in the years immediately following Masaccio's death. That the Florentines were prepared to award these hired mercenary captains with so great an honour as a mounted portrait on the walls of the Cathedral affords an interesting insight to the lingering insecurity that lay behind the superficial Florentine bravado. For like Venice, Florence always felt militarily vulnerable and was frequently forced to entrust the security and possessions of the state to the questionable skills and whimsical loyalties of these men—for instance in 1401 when the Milanese tried to besiege the city. Uccello's portrait (1436) is of *Sir John Hawkwood*, an Englishman who captained the Florentine army from 1377 to 1394 and was later made famous by Conan Doyle as the leader of the 'White Company'. Both paintings have twin points of perspective so that from beneath, that is from the eye level of the spectator, the horses seem to stand squarely on their plinths.

The Duomo was built in several different stages. The nave was completed by the mid-fourteenth century, though it was not until the early 1400s that any serious thought was given to the problem of roofing the crossing. It was only the absence of any serious alternative that drove the Cathedral authorities to attempt the beautiful and in every way stupendous dome that we see today. It was designed by Filippo Brunelleschi (1377–1446), the most human and likeable of the great early Renaissance figures. From the description in Vasari of his struggle to convince the authorities that his design was viable he emerges as one of the most fascinating artists of all time. Like Columbus trying to persuade the King of Spain that he could reach the east by sailing west, Brunelleschi struggled in vain for years to convince cautious committees that the dome could be built without structural centreing. And like Columbus he had to endure years of ridicule from those who thought his ideas absurd. Finally in 1420, his plans were approved and he began to build. For fifteen years the cupola rose in an ever-narrowing circle from its edge. As it went higher there were mass desertions by the workforce who were convinced that as it began to arch inwards it was certain to crash to the ground. But when finished it became the focal point of Florentine pride, as it still remains, a remarkable combination of engineering and architecture.

How did Brunelleschi know that his dome would stand? As its diameter is almost identical to that of the Pantheon it was once assumed that the vital inspiration was derived from a study of Roman architecture, but it is now thought that his basic structural principle came instead from the cupolas of the baptisteries in Florence and Pisa: a hollow vault with its inner and outer skin braced together to give added strength and to reduce the lateral thrusts that in Gothic cathedrals are absorbed by buttresses (6).

It is impossible to conceive how truly vast the cupola is without climbing to the first gallery of the drum (opening times, see p.229). Though the stairs are a little tiring there are few experiences in Florence that are more rewarding. As you look down over the crossing, the enormity of the space that Brunelleschi was required to vault becomes

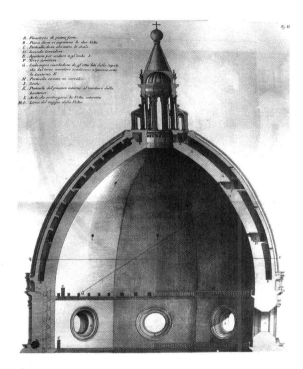

apparent. If you climb a little higher, between the two skins of the dome, you will appreciate the sophistication and the scale of the structure itself. The inner skin is thirteen feet thick and the outer seven. The eight marble ribs rising from each corner of the drum to the lantern are held together by three massive lateral stone and iron chains which Ruskin cited as an example of a permissible lapse from his doctrine of truth to materials. The weight of the dome is estimated to be around 25,000 tons.

It is from the gallery that one gets the best view of some of the most beautiful stained glass in Florence—the *occhi* or circular windows on each side of the drum designed by the most talented artists working in the first half of the fifteenth century. These were made, like the Uccello and Castagno frescoes in the nave, while the dome was under construction. The particularly lovely *Coronation of the Virgin* at the east side of the crossing (that is on the central axis of the Cathedral), is by Donatello. It is also the most appropriate place to recall Florence's only recorded 'murder in the Cathedral'—the attempt by the Pazzi family to oust the Medici in 1478. Giuliano de' Medici was stabbed in the breast at the western end of the octagonal sanctuary within the crossing. His luckier brother Lorenzo managed to escape to the safety of the Old Sacristy, which is to the northeast of the crossing. The murders benefited the Pazzi very little as their plot failed and the Pazzi were virtually wiped out by the violent recriminations of the 'Medici mafia'.

*   *   *

Some of the greatest works of art made to embellish the Duomo have since been removed to the Cathedral museum, the **Museo dell' Opera del Duomo**, a visit to which is an essential adjunct to any visit to the Cathedral itself. Finding it is very easy: we leave the Duomo by its southern door, turn left and walk to the far end of the Piazza del Duomo, then enter the courtyard immediately in front of us. (At Piazza del Duomo, no. 9).

Half way up the stairs stands the most pathetically moving and in terms of sculptural composition the most complicated of Michelangelo's *Pietàs* (c.1553). Made very near the end of his life, it was probably intended for his own tomb and according to Vasari, who was in the best position to know, the world-weary figure above Christ wearing a hood is a self-portrait. Michelangelo destroyed the group when he discovered a fault in the block but it was pieced together after his death.

The *Sala delle Cantorie* offers the luxury of a seat from which to enjoy the *Cantorie* (meaning singing galleries, although these were intended as organ lofts) removed from the Duomo. Made in the 1430s by Luca della Robbia (entrance wall, original panels below) and Donatello, they radiate a very different mood from the *Pietà*. Perhaps the more instantly likeable of the two is that by della Robbia, whose plump, happy, frolicking children play instruments, bash cymbals, sing and generally lighten the mood of a gallery that can feel cold and clinical. To appreciate the versatility of Donatello, look below the *Cantorie* at the *Penitent Magdalene*, probably but not certainly one of his later works and without doubt one of the most harrowing figure sculptures in Western art.

At either end of the room are the originals of the figures made by Donatello and others for the façade of the Campanile. These were made to be seen from a considerable distance, so their gestures and features are much exaggerated. The most powerful and the best known among them is Donatello's *Lo Zuccone* (1434–6), the bald-headed saint third from the right. In the far room are the originals of the Campanile plaques. The first room downstairs contains sculpture, mainly from the original façade of the Duomo. Some of them are by its architect, Arnolfo di Cambio. The two last rooms are dedicated to Brunelleschi and his dome.

*   *   *

If on emerging into the Museo dell' Opera del Duomo we walk down Via del Proconsolo and then take the second turning on the right into Via del Corso (noting on the opposite corner the large Palazzo built by the Pazzi shortly before their unfortunate plot) we will arrive in one of the most attractive, best preserved and colourful parts of old Florence. The streets around us, still densely populated, noisy, tall, busy, and rather claustro-phobic still look, if we overlook the modern shop-fronts, much as they did in Dante's time and, like other pockets of Florence, preserve a remarkable 'street life' though sandwiched between tourist traps.

Via S. Margherita (second on the left) leads to the famous **Casa di Dante** which, despite its name, is really only an elaborate restoration of a house in which Dante certainly did not live. But it is worth a quick look, for if Dante Alighieri (1265–1321)— the greatest and most influential Italian poet and one of the few figures from the high Middle Ages to have bequeathed a vivid impression of himself and his times to our day—did not live here then he lived somewhere very close by. In the church of S. Margherita (also in Via S. Margherita) is a monu-ment to Beatrice Portinari, the love of Dante's life whose early death inspired some of his finest passages and who will already be well known to those fortunate enough to have read any of Dante's work. On Piazza S. Martino, in front of the Casa di Dante, stands one of the finest remaining medieval towers in Florence, the Torre della Castagna. In Dante's lifetime towers such as this, impregnable family fortresses as much as a hun-dred feet high, must have dominated the centre of the city. In 1293 they were forcibly truncated to

about the present height of this tower and now only about thirty remain standing. Many of them can be seen in the surrounding streets. Off the piazza stands a small chapel, S. Martino del Vescovo, built in 1479 on the site of Dante's parish church. Its interior has frescoes by the workshop of Ghirlandaio.

If we return to Via del Corso, turn left and walk on a short way we reach Via dei Calzaioli, which runs from Piazza del Duomo to Piazza della Signoria; it is always full of people and is a particularly pleasant place to walk in the early evening. It was widened in the 1840s in the first of many well-intentioned but unfortunate acts of urban improvement that turned Florence from a sleepy Grand Ducal backwater untouched since 1600 into a modern city. Just to our west stands the hideous Piazza della Repubblica, the sight of which seems doubly painful when we realise that the oldest and most fascinating quarter of Florence, the Mercato Vecchio, was in 1888 demolished to create its site. Something approaching twenty per cent of the entire Florentine population is thought to have lived in or around

7

the Mercato Vecchio (7, 8). It was the red-light district, the ghetto, an artisans centre and the market all rolled into one. They existed in the kind of melancholy, shabby and picturesque poverty caught so well in the photographs opposite. A maze of tiny piazzas and churches, old houses and chapels, of peeling plaster and shabby booths, it delighted tourists but for the politicians of the brave new Italy it was a sordid reminder of a past they wished only to forget. So down it came, to the loud (if ineffective, for the heritage lobby was not quite what it is now) protests of the foreign community, and up went Piazza della Repubblica. It is worth looking at briefly because it represents so perfectly the brash insensitivity of Risorgimento Italy. There is something rather sad about the inscription on the triumphal arch at the western side of the Piazza which reads: *l'Antico centro della città da Secolare Squallore a Vita Nuova Restituita* (The ancient centre of the city after centuries of squalor has been restored to new life). One's jaundiced view of such wanton destruction at the hands of Risorgimento Italy's 'new men' might, however, be tempered by even

so dedicated a Florence-lover as Henry James, who notes in *Autumn in Florence* (1873): 'Florence today loses itself in dusty boulevards and smart *"beaux quartiers"*, such as Napoleon III and Baron Haussmann were to set the fashion of to a too medieval Europe—with the effect of some precious page of antique text swallowed up in a marginal commentary that smacks of the style of the newspaper. So much for what has happened on this side of that line of demarcation which, by an odd law, makes us, with our preference for what we are pleased to call the picturesque, object to such occurrences even *as* occurrences. The real truth is that objections are too vain, and that he would be too rude a critic here, just now, who shouldn't be in the humour to take the thick with the thin and to try at least to read something of the old soul in the new forms.' Not everyone, however, will be able to appreciate the Piazza della Repubblica with so broad a mind.

*   *   *

A little further down Via dei Calzaioli, on the right as you walk towards Piazza della Signoria, is one of the most unusual little churches in the world, **Or**

San Michele. It has a strange history full of irrationalities that have never been fully explained. Built in the third or fourth decades of the fourteenth century, the ground floor was originally an open loggia and in the two floors above grain was stored for use in times of emergency. Inside, it is still possible to see holes in the ceiling and chutes cut into columns used for transferring grain from one floor to another. Soon after the building was finished the ground floor was turned into a church and the loggia enclosed by enormous windows which, after a few years were, for no apparent reason, walled up.

It is partly because of these irrationalities that it has been called 'the most Florentine of Florentine buildings' and also because its undeniable beauty is derived from a peculiarly Florentine blend of the plain and the exotic. What might be a rather pedestrian rectangular block of *pietra forte* has a simple elegance that sets off florid window tracery of a quality not equalled in Tuscany (it is by an obscure fourteenth-century Florentine sculptor called Simone Talenti), ceramic medallions by Luca della Robbia and ornate niches, each allocated to a different trade guild responsible for their decoration.

It is the sculpture in these niches, and the niches themselves, that are the chief fascination of Or San Michele. Most of them were commissioned in the first half of the fifteenth century when the vigorous and emotionally expressive stylistic innovations of the early Renaissance begin to replace the more static work of the high Gothic. Since the guilds were extremely rich and powerful and since the quality of the decoration represented their own prestige, they commissioned the best artists of the day and encouraged them to work with the most expensive materials. Looking at one figure then another, you can begin to perceive the naked spirit of competition that existed in fifteenth-century Florence between both artists and their patrons and to appreciate the constant innovation that such competition bred. It is, then, the art-history teacher's dream, explaining the highly complicated development of Tuscan sculpture from 1350 to 1500 as a series of easy-to-grasp innovations that occur in a neat chronological order. Since these innovations are perhaps easier to perceive when explained, let us make a swift tour of the exterior.

The tabernacle to the far left on the Via dei Calzaioli façade was allotted to one of the most important of the major guilds or *Arti Maggiori*— the Calimae, representing the wool manufacturers and exporters. Their inevitable choice for a sculptor was Lorenzo Ghiberti whom they were already employing on the Baptistery doors. His *St John the Baptist* (1415) marks an important technical leap, though it makes few innovations in style—as in a figure made during the preceding century, St John is heavily bearded and immersed in a cloak, the rhythmical folds of which are not coordinated with the figure's anatomy. For this is the first life-size sculpture to be cast from bronze (at ostentatiously great cost) since antiquity.

To the right is a group of figures by Andrea Verrocchio (1435–88), a sculptor and painter much patronised by the Medici. If compared with the work of Ghiberti in the preceding niche, this two-figure group illustrates many of the innovations effected by Florentine sculptors during the course of the fifteenth century—their weight is dis-tributed in a more lifelike way and their clothes barely hide the musculation of the limbs. The tabernacle itself was designed not by Verrocchio but by Donatello for his gilded bronze *St Louis* (that has since found its way to the S. Croce museum). It demonstrates a profound understanding of the proportional rules governing the use of classical architecture and some suggest that it was designed with the advice of Filippo Brunelleschi. Higher on the wall is a ceramic roundel by della Robbia which incorporates that timeless motif of trade-unionism—the closed door.

The figure in the last tabernacle to the right on the Via dei Calzaioli façade is more than a century later. It was made in 1603 by Giambologna (1529–1608), the Flemish sculptor of genius who lived and worked in Florence for most of his life.

The third niche of the northern side contains the *Four Crowned Saints* (1415) by Nanni di Banco, a well known late Gothic sculptor whose most famous work is the Porta della Mandorla on the north side of the Duomo. Clearly 'closely inspired'—meaning copies—by Roman sculp-ture, they were used as models by Masaccio for figures in his fresco cycle in the Brancacci Chapel. Beside them is a copy of Donatello's *St George* (the original, made in 1417, was taken to the Bargello in 1888) who, poised on the balls of his feet, his face crossed by a frown, is the incarnation of the chivalric young knight. He represents the Florentine republic as it liked to see itself—young, gallant and triumphant against superior odds. It was equally attractive, for similar reasons, to Imperial England and hence the popularity of a similar or identical *St George* on so many First World War memorials. The predella beneath is usually held to be the first known example of the use of perspective in the Renaissance.

At the western end are two more bronze figures by Lorenzo Ghiberti cast about ten years later than the *St John*. They reflect the influence both of Ghiberti's visit to Rome and of his gradual absorption of the techniques and aims of Donatello. To the far left of the southern façade is perhaps the most important sculpture on the entire church. This is Donatello's *St Mark*, usually thought to be the first free-standing figure of the Renaissance. It was unveiled in 1411, when the typical Florentine free-standing statue was characterised by *St Luke* by Nicolo Lamberti in the next niche to the right, with a head too large and arms too short for the body, and a face that wears an expression of vacuous piety. In contrast *St Mark* is full of life, his weight is carried through one leg, his cloak follows the movement of his body and his face has an intelligent, serious look. Donatello uses various techniques to make the figure appear more life-like—the neck is longer than it should be to compensate for being seen from below and he stands on a cushion in order to emphasise his weight.

If we step inside Or San Michele from Via dei Calzaioli, immediately in front of us is an altar that Edward Hutton, expressing the opinions of many others, was moved to call 'the loveliest of its kind in Italy' and 'perhaps the most beautiful example of the Italian Gothic manner in existence'. It was commissioned (from Andrea Orcagna) in 1349 by the survivors of the Black Death of the previous year which is thought to have eliminated about a quarter of the population. Christians of the Middle Ages sincerely believed that such natural disasters were divine retribution for mortal sin and it was their understandable desire to avoid another plague, which must explain why the Florentines, famous then as now for the tightness of their purse strings, spent so much money on it. Every part of its surface is elaborately decorated, either with carving, inlay or statuettes. Around the base are reliefs of the *Life of the Virgin* and facing the door is a relief of the *Assumption*. It remains, however, another of Or San Michele's mysteries as to why they decided to erect it here, where it seems so uncomfortably cramped. The painting of the Madonna is contemporary with the altar and has been attributed to Bernardo Daddi. On the second altar to the right is a statue of the *Madonna and Child* by Francesco da Sangallo. On the vaults in the opposite corner from the entrance you can see the chutes used for bagging grain. After looking quickly at all of these, and not forgetting to admire the Gothic stained glass or the frescoes on the walls, we emerge from Or San Michele and walk to Via Calimala, at its western end, which leads to the straw market. Here we may or may not feel moved to buy one of the exciting things there offered for sale or to make a wish while touching the snout of the famous 'lucky' bronze boar (cast by Giambologna from a classical sculpture in the Medici collection) before turning left into the Piazza della Signoria, the subject of the next chapter. By now we are sure to feel like sitting down and drinking a cup of coffee. This is extremely convenient, for to our right is one of the best cafés in the world, Rivoire, from which we can relish the atmosphere and admire the buildings of the largest and grandest Florentine piazza.

Map 2
Piazza della Signoria

1. Café Rivoire
2. Tribunale della Mercanzia
3. Loggia della Signoria (dei Lanzi)
4. Palazzo Uguccioni
5. Palazzo della Signoria (Vecchio)
6. *David*
7. *Neptune*
8. *Hercules and Cacus*
9. *Perseus*
10. *Rape of the Sabine*
11. Equestrian Monument to Cosimo I
12. Raccolta d'Arte Moderna Alberto della Ragione

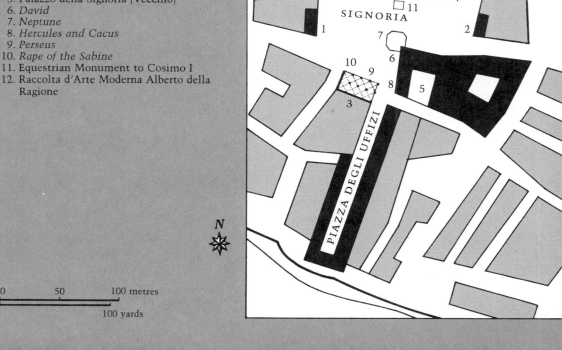

PIAZZA DELLA SIGNORIA

PIAZZA DEGLI UFFIZI

N

0   50   100 metres

100 yards

2

THE PIAZZA
—and—
PALAZZO DELLA SIGNORIA

✤ From a table outside Rivoire (1) we can look across the Piazza della Signoria from the same position as that chosen by Bernardo Bellotto for his painting (9). The topography has changed a little over the last two centuries—the church and most of the buildings on the northern side of the Piazza have disappeared and there is a nineteenth-century mock Renaissance building behind us—but for all this the Piazza today enjoys the same curiously shabby, informal charm evoked by Bellotto. Though it compares rather poorly with the great piazzas of other Italian cities—one thinks of the stupendous Campo in Siena or of Piazza S. Marco in Venice—it is a fine spectacle capable of carrying the historical imagination of the visitor, particularly if he or she is in a romantic mood, far into the past.

It has been said that if the marbled buildings of the Piazza del Duomo are the glittering façade to the history of the Florentine republic, then those of the Piazza della Signoria represent its less glamorous backstage reality. For not one among them appears to make the slightest effort to conform with or concede to another and in this instance at least they all too faithfully echo the state of perpetual conflict that characterises Florentine history during the later medieval period. But some of them are very fine: the

Tribunale della Mercanzia (2), the court for business affairs at the eastern end, dates from the mid-fourteenth century. From close to it appears more unusual than from a distance because the façade is embellished with fine terracotta heraldic arms. Then to the right is the superb **Loggia della Signoria** (3), an elegant combination of Gothic vaulting and classical arches, built between 1376 and 1382 as a raised platform from which the Priors could address a *parlamento* or meeting of the male citizens. In the sixteenth century, long after the Republican spirit had disappeared, and the possibility of a *parlamento* of the citizens being called must have seemed as remote as the fall of the Medici, it was used as a shelter by the Grand Duke's praetorian guard of Swiss Lancers, hence its present name, the **Loggia dei Lanzi**. Michelangelo admired it so much that he urged Cosimo I to repeat its arches all around the Piazza.

The most beautiful building on the Piazza is on its north side—**Palazzo Uguccioni** (4) which is mid-sixteenth century and so heavily Roman in character that some scholars have suggested that it may have been built after designs by Raphael.

Opposite, dominating the Piazza, is that massive urban fortress, the **Palazzo della Signoria** (5) also known as the **Palazzo Vecchio** and at one time, just to make things more complicated, as the Palazzo Gran Ducale. It was begun in 1295 and finished in the early fourteenth century, though large-scale additions were made in the late 1400s. It is the largest, in some ways the most impressive, but hardly the most elegant example of secular architecture in Tuscany of the later medieval period. The Signoria's builders seem to have displayed little grasp of the logic for which their descendants were to become famous—no room within the building is a true square, and the façades are asymmetric owing to the determination of the Guelphs not to build on land once owned by a Ghibelline. It might have been removed or perhaps altered by one of the enlightened Grand Dukes had the solidity of its construction not rendered demolition virtually impossible. The walls are metres thick, while the tower rests on a column of solid stone that rises within the building to the height of the crenellations.

For about two centuries the Palazzo della Signoria was the nerve-centre of Florentine government. The Republic's complex and virtually unworkable constitution was aimed at avoiding the seizure of power by a dictator. A committee of nine Priors was elected every two months to form a Signoria, but as no Prior was allowed to serve more than once every five years the inevitable result was that the state's domestic and foreign affairs were hopelessly mismanaged and at regular intervals the Signoria was obliged to accept the steering hand of and domination by families of considerable political acumen—such as the Medici—who by skilful manipulation of the constitution managed to govern Florence virtually as they wished for sixty years during the fifteenth century.

If the system was not efficient, neither was it democratic, since the elections were carefully controlled so that only a small proportion of citizens, usually members of the elite two or three hundred families who controlled the economy, ever came to serve as Priors in the first place. During their term of office these Priors were obliged to live virtually as prisoners inside the Palazzo della Signoria, the idea being that if they were kept isolated from the population they might remain immune from bribery or intimidation. They all slept in one room on the second floor attended by male servants dressed in green livery. It is not easy to picture their existence, but not hard to see why so many regarded the office as a time-consuming burden. The most important part of their duties, certainly in the eyes of their fellow citizens, was the assessment of individuals for taxation. Though surprisingly little is understood about the financial aspects of earlier Florentine history, one thing is certain—that a large proportion of the state's employees were tax collectors, which can only mean that the Florentines, like their contemporary descendants, while accepting the obligation to pay taxes, could never escape the conviction that they were contributing rather more than their fair share.

The Piazza is more famous for its sculpture than for its buildings. Along the façade of the Signoria and inside the Loggia dei Lanzi you see good examples of the work of the greatest sixteenth-century Florentine sculptors. The pleasure that they impart will be all the greater for those who have read the autobiography of Benvenuto Cellini (1500–71) and can appreciate the atmosphere of cut-throat competition in which they were made and commissioned.

Michelangelo's *David* (6) (now replaced by a copy, the original having been taken in great pomp to the Galleria dell' Accademia in 1873 on a specially constructed tramline) was originally intended for the Piazza del Duomo, but it so impressed his contemporaries, who saw it as a symbol of the triumph of republican values over tyranny, that it was installed before the seat of government. To produce a work of sculpture that would rival or outshine Michelangelo's *David* became the obsession of succeeding generations of Florentine artists, particularly of the three leading sculptors in Florence under Cosimo I who fought bitterly amongst each other for his patronage—Benvenuto Cellini, Bartolomeo Ammanati (1511–92) and Baccio Bandinelli (1493–1560). Around the *David* we see their very different attempts.

Jutting out from the corner of the Palazzo is Ammanati's *Neptune* (7) (1560–75), perhaps not adequately engulfed in torrents of white spray to achieve its full effect but nevertheless impressive. Four horses, two of them in purplish marble, charge through the waters pulling a chariot from which Neptune rules the Seas. Faintly pompous and not oversubtly symbolic of Cosimo's naval triumphs, it was dubbed with a derogatory nickname—*Il Biancone*, or the great white hulk—almost as soon as it was finished in 1575. Neptune's size and colour strikes an intentional contrast with the lounging, semi-human bronze figures around the base sprouting horns or with hoofs for feet. These are mainly the work of Ammanati's assistants, who included Giambologna.

However rude the Florentines may have been about the *Neptune* it was not subjected to the sort of vitriol aimed at *Hercules and Cacus* (8) (1534) by Bandinelli. Though intended as a pendant to the *David*, it seems painfully crude and stylised in comparison. Bandinelli's arch enemy was Cellini who, making the sort of tactful and conciliatory gesture for which he is famous, described *Hercules and Cacus* to Cosimo I, in the presence of Bandinelli, as resembling 'an old sack full of melons'.

You will forgive Cellini all the pomposity, the immodesty and self-importance of his autobiography when you turn to his wonderful *Perseus* (9) (1545–60), which stands in the Loggia dei Lanzi. It is difficult to read the pages describing the casting of the figure without excitement. After a long build-up, which describes the frustrating years spent winning the commission and convincing Cosimo that such a complex figure could be made in bronze—he modelled the *Perseus* first in clay and then in wax—he provides a graphic description of the difficulties experienced during casting. Everything that can go wrong does go wrong—he catches a fever, the workshop catches fire, he runs out of firewood and then discovers he has too little bronze to fill the cast. With characteristic modesty he describes how he saved the day by throwing his pewter plates into the kiln. Recent metallurgical analysis of the *Perseus* seems to confirm that this part of the story, at least, is absolutely true.

Unlike Bandinelli and Ammanati, Cellini's training was as a goldsmith, and much of the effect of the *Perseus* is dependent on its fine and sometimes revoltingly gruesome detail, such as the blood as it slowly drips from the Medusa's truncated head, or the elaborate winged helmet and shoes, though it is a strong composition and the gentle virility of Perseus himself is perfectly set off by the writhing Medusa at his feet.

To either side of the steps in the second bay are two lions—the one to the right is Roman, the one to the left is a sixteenth-century copy. In the third bay to the right stands the *Rape of the Sabine* (10) (1583) by Giambologna, the greatest sculptor of the next generation. He contrasts the actions of three quite different physiques—an old man, a virile youth and a voluptuous woman. It has all the springing action and turning movement that Bernini was to perfect in the next century, and unlike the *Perseus* it is designed without a fixed viewpoint, the intention being that from every angle it should appear in perfect proportion. Behind is his less famous *Hercules and the Centaur*. The five *Empresses* or *Goddesses* along the back wall are Roman copies of Greek originals.

Giambologna's *Equestrian Monument to Cosimo I* (11) (1595) should really be seen from the Uffizi, from where he is framed by the mirrored façades of a building that was intended to symbolise his princely rationalisation of an urban republic into a well organised modern state. It has a certain art-historical importance as the first mounted equestrian monument to be made since the fifteenth century. The relief panels at its base are of great quality and describe an horrific episode that made Cosimo I the envy of every Prince in Italy—the annexation of Siena after a long siege during which forty per cent of that city's population died resisting the combined Spanish and Florentine armies.

* * *

Now for the **interior** of the Palazzo della Signoria. This may surprise the visitor since almost all of the original decoration from the Palazzo's days as the bastion of the Republic were destroyed by Cosimo I who in 1540, three years after his accession, moved in and established it as his court. Employing a number of artists among whom the most important and productive, if not the most

talented, was Giorgio Vasari (author of the famous *Lives of the Artists*), he then began a systematic programme of redecoration.

As the Prince of a new 'upstart' dynasty Cosimo (10) was painfully aware of his family's shaming commercial origins and the purpose of his vast scheme of repainting was simple—to provide the Medici with a history, to celebrate the brilliance of their past, to efface all reminders of the Medicean commercial origins and to provide a setting for a brilliant new court equipped with every aristocratic trapping down to jesters and dwarfs. Thus every painting in the Palazzo, however small, however out of the way, is a carefully thought-out celebration either of Cosimo himself, his biblical counterparts or of his ancestors. Though we may, after a time, find this theme faintly tedious and feel rather less enthusiastic about Cosimo and his achievements than perhaps we should, and though Vasari's paintings often leave much to be desired, his palazzo is a wonderful evocation of a sinister sixteenth-century world of Machiavellian intrigue. There is also much pleasure to be derived from observing the skill with which Cosimo uses art for purposes of dynastic propaganda.

The decoration of the first courtyard is by Vasari and his assistants. The faded murals are of towns under Austrian control and were painted to honour the arrival of Francesco I's Austrian bride in 1565, the first in a series of very grand but ultimately disastrous Medici marriages. Vasari's monumental staircase (first buy a ticket on the ground floor) leads to the vast Salone dei Cinquecento, built in the last decade of the fifteenth century to house the Consiglio Maggiore—the enlarged representative government of Florence's penultimate republic. Here too the Italian Parliament sat from 1865 to 1870 when Florence was capital of the newly united Italy. Though enormous, the room is far from magnificent. Leonardo and Michelangelo were commissioned in 1503 to paint vast frescoes on the two long walls but Michelangelo's never went further than its cartoon (though that was perhaps the single most influential drawing of its generation), and Leonardo's crumbled after a few years because of his experimental and disastrous fresco technique.

10

The present frescoes were painted in 1563–5 by Vasari and represent the Florentine victories over Siena and Pisa. They are some of his least successful paintings. The wild crush of horses and men, rather than creating the intended effect of seething movement, dissolves into a confusing, uncoordinated muddle. His ceiling paintings are more successful, particularly *Cosimo Planning the Sienese War* (in an octagonal frame) which alludes to the prince's military prowess.

At the far side of the room is a two-figure group by Michelangelo called *Victory*. The remainder of the sculpture in the Salone dei Cinquecento is by Michelangelo's less distinguished contemporaries Bandinelli and Vincenzo de' Rossi. You may be amused by the contortions of the latter's *Hercules and Diomedes* which stands to the right of *Victory*.

The Studiolo of Francesco I, perhaps the most fascinating room in the Palazzo, is entered through the glass door at the right end of the entrance wall. Windowless, small, claustrophobic and overflowing with the highly finished, subtly erotic work of the best later sixteenth-century

11

painters and sculptors, it provides a tantalising glimpse into the mind and life of the most complex and morose of the Grand Dukes. The antithesis of his father Cosimo, Francesco I was solitary, remote and reclusive (11). Detesting court life, he withdrew to ornate bolt-holes—like this or his Tribuna in the Uffizi, where he would spend days on his own conducting strange scientific experiments.

The paintings in the Studiolo explore different aspects of Man's relationship to Nature. The programme was devised by Raffaello Borghini, the leading intellectual of the time, and executed (1569–73) by a team of painters and sculptors that included Vasari, Bronzino, Allori, Giambologna and Ammanati. In the lunettes at either end are portraits by Bronzino of Francesco's mother and father. Around the walls are a series of wonderful paintings. Two of the best are (furthest to the left) Vasari's *Perseus and Andromeda* and (second from the end) Alessandro Allori's *Pearl Fishermen*. Both have a quality of subtle eroticism echoed by Ammanati's snake-hipped *Venus* and Giambologna's *Apollo*. The lower row of pictures

conceal cupboards where Francesco kept his most precious and rare possessions. The Studiolo was dismantled in the late eighteenth century—its pictures were taken to the Uffizi and its bronzes to the Bargello. It was only through the action of an effective and cultured mayor in 1907 that these were retrieved and its undeniably sinister atmosphere reconstructed.

To the other side of the Salone dei Cinquecento are five rooms (painted by Vasari and his assistants, 1555–62) which provide a graphic illustration of the sophistication of Medicean dynastic propaganda. Each room celebrates the life of a different member of the Medici, touching only on the high points of that character's career. The series begins with the Sala di Cosimo 'pater patriae' who is represented as he returns from exile in 1434 to a tumultuous welcome, thus establishing the family's political fortunes. You then move on to the Sala di Lorenzo il Magnifico, then to two larger rooms celebrating the lives of Leo X and Clement VII, the Medici Popes, then enter the climax to the series, the Sala di Cosimo I, dedicated to the life and achievements of the incumbent Grand Duke, who is seen apotheosised on the ceiling.

Vasari's frescoes are more interesting from an historical than an artistic point of view, particularly the *Siege of Florence* by Charles V in the Sala di Clemente VII, and *Cosimo I Surrounded by his Artists* in the Sala di Cosimo, which alludes to the Prince's role as patron. Vasari and Cellini are to his right and Bandinelli to his left, but there is one conspicuous absence—Michelangelo—who stubbornly refused every bribe to return to his native city while it was ruled by Cosimo I.

To the left of the landing at the top of the stairs are a set of dull rooms called the Quartiere degli Elementi, worth walking through only to reach the Terrazzo di Saturno which overlooks the best prospect of Florence. If you turn the other way from the landing and walk down the corridor you reach Cosimo's wife's apartments, the Quartiere di Eleonora, which are interesting principally for the paintings (1540–5) in the Cappella di Eleonora, her private chapel, by Agnolo Bronzino. Though known principally for his coldly incisive portraits, Bronzino is also a religious painter of great merit.

Inevitably enough the paintings correspond to Cosimo's overall allegorical scheme. The walls and ceiling depict *Scenes from the Story of Moses*, an attractive biblical counterpart to Cosimo, who saw himself as leading the Florentines from the wilderness of Republican government.

Cosimo was adequately sensitive to leave the decoration of the fine Sala dei Gigli, further on, virtually untouched. The doorcases, the gold ceiling and the cornice date from between 1476 and 1480 and were made by the Da Maiano brothers. The frescoes were painted in 1481–5 by Domenico and Davide Ghirlandaio. Donatello's macabre *Judith and Holofernes* (1456–60) was installed here in 1980 as a refuge from the Piazza's destructive pigeons.

The Sala dell' Udienza next door was also decorated by the Da Maiano brothers, though now what catches the eye are its clever, lively murals (1550–60) by Cecchino Salviati which abound in references to antiquity, particularly in *Peace Conquering War* on the left wall. In the Cancelleria there is a bust and a portrait of the man who symbolises, more than any other, the scheming

Renaissance statecraft at which Cosimo I excelled, Niccolo Machiavelli (1469–1527).

Though his name has become synonymous with his age, Machiavelli was a surprisingly conventional character who displayed few of the vices or indeed of the skills that he describes and praises in his books. His career was short and relatively undistinguished. It began in 1498 when he entered the bureaucracy of the Republic, working as a secretary to the Council of Ten, which dealt with military and foreign affairs. It ended in 1512 when the Medici again took up the reins of government and dismissed Machiavelli, who was forced to retire to the country and write the books and plays which, though now famous, were not particularly successful in his lifetime. He died, disappointed and unfulfilled, in 1527 and could never have guessed that his work, in particular *The Prince* which was not published until 1532, would win him such fame.

The Palazzo della Signoria was not a jail or a criminal court, though in the tower (not open to the public) there is a small cell called, with a sardonic humour that is typically Florentine, the *alberghetto* or 'little hotel'. Here important prisoners were occasionally held while the Priors deliberated on their fate. This was where, in the same year that Machiavelli joined the Republic's bureaucracy, the fanatical Dominican Fra Girolamo Savonarola spent his last months and 'confessed' to heresy under torture before being executed then burnt in the Piazza below. (The exact spot is marked by a plaque in the paving, to the west of the equestrian statue of Cosimo I.) A fifteenth-century Ayatollah, Savonarola stands for everything that Machiavelli does not. Following the expulsion of the Medici in 1494, he subjected the Florentines to an invigorating Puritan purge that culminated in bonfires of paintings, furniture and fine clothes. After four years the patience of his following melted away and he ended up on the stake.

The stairs lead down to the exit, though on the mezzanine those lucky enough to retain any mental vigour after the rigours of the Palazzo will enjoy the **Collezione Loeser**, left to Florence in 1928 by Charles Loeser, one of the most interesting of the connoisseur-collectors living in

The Loggia dei Lanzi

Florence at the turn of the century. He had a good eye and good taste, and, as the principal heir to Macy's Department store, ample private means with which to indulge his consuming passion— collecting works of art. Though he left the finest part of his collection, twenty Cézannes bought from the Parisian dealer Vollard for next to nothing in the 1880s, to the White House (which turned them down) there are several objects here of great interest, particularly the *Portrait of Laura Battifieri* by Bronzino. Loeser himself was convinced that the terracotta horse was by Leonardo and that the marble tondo of the Madonna was by Michelangelo, though he has never been supported in these opinions.

If we are still feeling energetic we could end the morning with a visit to the **Raccolta d'Arte Moderna Alberto della Ragione** (12) on the north side of the Piazza della Signoria; it houses a collection of Italian twentieth-century paintings which make a pleasant change of scene after our overdose of Cosimo's sometimes verbose court art. The restaurants at the far end of the Piazza are surprisingly cheap and good, particularly the pizzeria beside Palazzo Uguccioni and the Trattoria Cavallino, with a fine view down through the Uffizi.

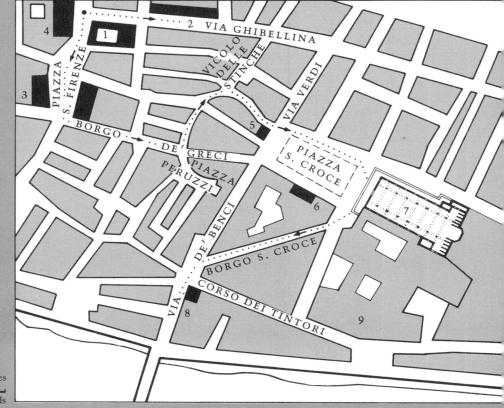

Map 3
The Bargello and
S. Croce

1. Bargello
2. Palazzo Borghese
3. Palazzo Gondi
4. Badia
5. Palazzo Seristori
6. Palazzo dell' Antella
7. Santa Croce
8. Fondazione Horne
9. Biblioteca Nazionale

2 VIA GHIBELLINA

VICOLO DELLE STINCHE

VIA VERDI

PIAZZA S. FIRENZE

BORGO DE' GRECI

PIAZZA PERUZZI

PIAZZA S. CROCE

VIA DE' BENCI

BORGO S. CROCE

CORSO DEI TINTORI

N

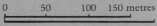

0   50   100   150 metres

200 yards

3

THE BARGELLO
—*and*—
S. CROCE

✤ It seems to me strangely ironic that the **Bargello**, one of the grimmest Florentine buildings and certainly that with the most sinister history, should now house the most beautiful collection of Renaissance sculpture in the world. For the greater part of its 700-odd-year history it has served a less glamorous role as the city prison for which purpose, if one were to judge by its exterior alone, few buildings seem so admirably suited. The rooms which today contain the loveliest and most civilised Florentine figurative art are silent witnesses to some of the least civilised and lovely acts of the society that created them. Here, from the early years of the fourteenth century, the chief magistrate or Podestà lived among his police and prisoners, administering a code of justice that would appear harsh even to Judge Jeffreys. A man convicted of sodomy could be burnt at the stake, as could a Jew convicted of sleeping with a Christian prostitute. A thief might escape with a fine but if it was not paid he might have a foot or a hand cut off. Confessions were frequently extracted by torture and the Bargello housed a torture chamber as recently as 1786. Executions were generally carried out in the courtyard, and it was here in 1849 that the Austrians shot Italian nationalists. It may interest the more macabre to know that Leonardo once stood outside the

12

Bargello and sketched the decomposing bodies of men hung from its windows after the Pazzi plot. Andrea del Castagno, the great early fifteenth-century painter, decorated part of the exterior of the tower with frescoes of the tortured corpses of the condemned. But today there is nothing to be seen of them, and there is nothing, in fact, to remind the visitor that anything unpleasant happened here at all. However hellish it must once have seemed to its prisoners, the Bargello is today the most captivating and delightful place in Florence and certainly my own favourite among all the city's museums. (12) Let us delay no longer and begin our visit.

Entering the courtyard from the street (pausing to buy tickets on the way), the visitor experiences a pleasant surprise, for to describe the contrast between the exterior and interior of the Bargello as 'striking' is to say too little. If from without it looks grim and menacing, the interior is wildly romantic. The walls are covered in a mosaic of armorial plaques in stone erected to the memory of the different Podestà (one of them was called Bargello, and hence the building's name); the

tower shoots up into the sky and a staircase (built in the mid-fourteenth century and therefore slightly later than the rest of the building) leads to a shadowy loggia. This could be the setting for some particularly melodramatic scene in George Eliot's *Romola*. It would be nice to say that all of what we see around us dates from the mid-thirteenth century when the Bargello (or Palazzo del Popolo as it was originally called) was originally built, but it has to be admitted that a good deal of its most admired features results from a skilful restoration carried out just prior to the building's conversion into a museum in the 1860s. Photograph 13 (overleaf) gives us some idea of how it looked before that time.

Most of the sculpture around the courtyard is sixteenth-century. Immediately to the right after the entrance is a faintly verbose figure of *Cosimo I as a Roman Emperor* by Vincenzo Danti (1530–76), a Perugian sculptor who pursued a successful career in Florence until the rise of Giambologna. Lining the back wall (with the exception of the piece in the left corner) are a series of statues made by Ammanati for a fountain planned to embellish

the Salone dei Cinquecento in the Palazzo della Signoria. Giambologna's giant *Oceanus* (in the far corner) was originally made for the Boboli Gardens but was endlessly moved from villa to villa by the Medici who seem to have had a particular fondness for it. The wrought-iron lantern on the left wall is an attractive survival from the sixteenth century. The charming *Fisherboy* (1877) is by a talented Neapolitan late nineteenth-century sculptor called Vincenzo Gemito. The cannon comes from the battery in Leghorn but has no especially romantic history attached to it, indeed it has probably never been fired in a battle.

After a walk around the courtyard casting admiring glances in every direction the conscientious visitor will enter Room I, at the far side of the courtyard, containing some early Tuscan sculpture of real quality. The loveliest objects in the room are both early to mid-fourteenth century— the *Three Acolytes* around a column by Arnolfo di Cambio (who is more famous as the architect of the Duomo and S. Croce), and Tino di Camaino's *Madonna and Child*. These are of a roughly similar date to the *Maestà* by Cimabue and Giotto

that now hang in the Uffizi.

From here we move to the first floor by walking up the staircase in the courtyard. If we turn right at the top we shall walk straight into the stupendous Sala del Consiglio Generale, once the courtroom of the Podestà, which is filled by some of the greatest early Renaissance sculpture. Many will agree that the things around us are some of the most lovely ever produced by Western civilisation. 'Early fifteenth-century Florentine sculptors', said Walter Pater, 'share with the paintings of Botticelli and the churches of Brunelleschi that profound expressiveness, that intimate impress of an indwelling soul that is the peculiar fascination of the art of Italy in that century.' Their work has a tender, subtle grace as difficult to describe in words as it must be to achieve in the materials from which it is made, but which is brought wonderfully to life amongst the soaring Gothic vaults and acres of plain white wall of this magnificent room.

This room contains examples of the work of all the most important and talented early Renaissance sculptors—Luca della Robbia, Desiderio da

Settignano, Bernardo Rossellino, Agostino di Duccio, Mino da Fiesole and the outstanding genius among them all—Donatello (1386–1466), who, despite his vast importance in the history of Florentine art, remains a mysterious figure. His life and work have resisted a definitive chronological or stylistic classification. Despite monograph after monograph, his artistic personality remains an enigma and parts of his long life a mystery. As is the case with some other great artists, his work can only be understood as a series of inspirations that lead him, at regular intervals, in totally new directions. The range of his inspiration and of his talent is well illustrated by the different examples of his work in this room. It can be difficult to believe, for instance, that the *Atys Amor*, a camp little cupid, is by the same hand as the sombre relief of the *Crucifixion* or the gallant *St George* mounted in a niche on the far wall. The precise chronological order in which these things were made is not certain, though the marble *David* (1408–9), is thought to be Donatello's earliest work. *St George* was completed in 1416, when Donatello was thirty years old. It was made for Or

San Michele from where it was removed (to an international howl of protest) in 1888.

The best known and most enigmatic of Donatello's works—the bronze *David*—is also the least well documented. A work of extraordinary originality, it was the first free-standing nude figure to be made for a millennium. Scores of researchers working through the Florentine archives over the last few decades have failed to turn up any concrete information about when or for whom it was made. The more cautious catalogues of Donatello's work only date it within a span of twenty-five years, from 1430 to 1455. The subject of numerous different interpretations, it has been taken as proof of Donatello's presumed homosexuality and as a symbol of youthful republicanism in the tradition of his *St George* and Michelangelo's *David*. It may be both, but more obviously it is an essay in physical perfection and one of the most sensual nudes ever made. It looks alluring from most angles, but particularly so if seen from the right-hand side. A large hat accentuates the tilt of the head, his face wears a distant and charming smile and the light, striking from above, melts the body into a series of glistening bronze curves. He imparts to the figure an almost incredible softness and realism not simply by adding frankly realistic details but by providing contrast with the tangled mess of Goliath's hair and the sharp, tooled lines on the top of David's boots. Like the *Amor* at the other end of the room the *David* has a strange, indefinable erotic energy to which most visitors to the Bargello can feel some kind of response. 'It is a common experience today in front of Donatello's works to feel that he is an artist in our modern sense, a sculptor whose work results from reconstructible thought processes,' says Sir John Pope-Hennessy. And this is never more true than when standing in front of the *David*.

On the right wall hang the famous trial panels representing the *Sacrifice of Isaac* made for the Baptistery doors competition of 1401 by Filippo Brunelleschi and Lorenzo Ghiberti, perhaps the most overdiscussed works of art of the Florentine Renaissance. Laboured descriptions of these two panels and of the competition which brought them into being contribute some of the dreariest pages to any textbook on Italian sculpture.

Ghiberti's, to the left, was judged superior, possibly on technical grounds, since, unlike that by Brunelleschi, it is cast as a single panel. The relief panel between them—a writhing mêlée of horses and men in the *Battle Scene* by Giovanni di Bertoldo—is one of the finest things in the Bargello. Not a great deal is known about the life of Bertoldo, except that as the pupil of Donatello and the early master of Michelangelo he provides a link between the two greatest sculptors of the Renaissance.

Walking from the Sala del Consiglio to the Loggia, we move from the fifteenth to the sixteenth century, a period of momentous political change in which Florence was transformed from a Republic to a Principate and Florentine art ceased to be the propaganda of republics and the Church and became instead the propaganda of princes and kings. Here we see some of the best and most obviously and eccentrically 'princely' work of one of the great court artists of the sixteenth century—Giambologna, perhaps the most important European sculptor between Michelangelo and Bernini. Born a Fleming (and originally called Jean de Boulogne which was later Italianised to Giambologna) he came to Italy in search of work, arriving in Florence in the 1550s. He was soon taken up by the Medici and from about 1575 until his death in 1608 he was their court sculptor—much to the envy of other princes and kings who competed for his work just as keenly as they did, a generation later, for the paintings of his fellow countryman Peter Paul Rubens.

At the near end of the Loggia are some of his most likeable if least 'important' works—a series of bronze animals made for the gardens of Medici villas. These probably look rather less exotic to us than they must have to a patron of the sixteenth century. The playfully hideous turkey is the first representation of the species in Western art since, despite its misleading name, it can only have arrived in Europe a few years earlier from the New World. Though today he is better known for his large monumental pieces, like the superb *Rape of the Sabine* in the Piazza della Signoria, in his own day Giambologna's international reputation was based on the extraordinarily high quality of his small bronzes. Many of them, like the original

version of the vigorous yet supremely elegant 'flying' *Mercury* (1564) at the other end of the Loggia were commissioned by the Medici as diplomatic gifts to various European rulers. A study in the perfect balance between vertical and horizontal movement, it proved immensely popular and its copies had 'flown' to galleries all over Europe by the end of the seventeenth century.

Like Rubens, Giambologna owed much of his success to his efficiency. He was able to produce work on time and in quantity for demanding patrons by organising his studio like a small-scale factory. He himself would model the original perhaps half a dozen times, in clay and wax, then entrust the fnished model to his assistants to execute. In the final stages he might alter the face or hands, just as Rubens or Titian might add the finishing touches to a canvas.

The rest of this floor has been used as a convenient parking space for collections that the city has gratefully received over the last hundred years but not really known what to do with. Some of it is of exceptional interest, particularly the collection of decorative arts donated in the 1880s by a fanatical French collector called Louis Carrand. Though very little of his collection is Florentine, for some reason he seems to have thought Florence the city best qualified to receive it on his death. This occupies most of the remaining rooms on the first floor. In Room 10 our attention may be caught by his fine collection of ivories, perhaps by the twelfth-century *Madonna and Child* or by a series of small late-medieval French panels depicting *Scenes from the Castle of Love* which, appropriately enough, evoke a world of chivalry and courtly romance, before we arrive in Room 8 which was the Podestà's long, vaulted salone. His chapel, at the near end of the room, was the scene of great excitement in 1841. At the instigation of an enthusiastic group of medievalists, led by a lawyer from Georgia called Richard Henry Wilde (who wrote the *Life and Times of Dante* in a volume of several hundred thousand words that omits the majority of the 'life' but goes into much detail about the 'times'), a series of frescoes was discovered beneath an inch and a half of whitewash. They were immediately pronounced to be by Giotto, and the figure just to the left of the centre in a red cap was identified as a portrait of Dante (**14**), though a clumsy restorer managed to remove his right eye while pulling out a nail. Is this really a portrait of Dante? It seems unlikely, since he was exiled from Florence under threat of death, that the Podestà could have wished to see his portrait in his private chapel. The paintings are now universally catalogued as 'School of Giotto', one way of saying that scholars cannot make up their minds who painted them.

Enthusiasts for ceramics will doubtless return to Room 12 to admire the Medici collection of majolica before taking the stairs to the second floor where we will find ourselves surrounded by the later work of a dynasty of Florentine sculptors as remarkable for their creative talent as for their healthy business sense—the della Robbia. Luca della Robbia (1400–82) was a highly accomplished and successful sculptor in marble and bronze before a technical breakthrough, made in about 1440, led him to realise that it was possible to apply the same coloured enamel glazes used on majolica to sculpture modelled in terracotta, rendering it impervious to damp and (as was pro-

ved during the flood of 1966) virtually indestructible. The discovery, allowing him to produce a durable, as well as much cheaper, alternative to sculpture made from conventional materials, became a closely guarded secret of the family workshop. Its obvious commercial possibilities were fully exploited by his nephew Andrea della Robbia (1435–1525) whose sons continued to use it until the mid-sixteenth century.

The beauty and charm of the della Robbias' work is its simplicity. Combining the advantages both of sculpture and of painting, it makes no attempt at visual illusion or effects of deep perspective, but achieves a serene poetry with a palette of lovely blues (which Pater described as resembling 'fragments of the milky sky itself'), yellows and greens, applied to bunches of fruit, to clothes and backgrounds, surrounding the white figures and causing them to stand out with a radiance that is almost celestial.

Around the walls of the first room at the top of the stairs, however, we see some of their last and least appealing productions. Mostly they are the work of Andrea's son Giovanni della Robbia and

14

made in the sixteenth century when quality had clearly been sacrificed to quantity. By the 1520s their family 'shop' could have been more accurately described as the family production line, from which rolled literally hundreds of altarpieces and tabernacles of the Madonna for churches all over Italy and as far away as the Low Countries. They were often made (as are most of the examples in this room) from hundreds of different pieces of coloured porcelain so that they could be more easily transported to the point of commission. In the smaller room to the left are earlier and much more beautiful examples of their work such as Andrea della Robbia's *Bust of a Young Boy* or the lovely *Portrait of a Young Lady* in a circular frame which is usually attributed to Luca della Robbia.

Room 14, full of portrait busts, is my own favourite in the Bargello. Here, surrounded by the patrons of the fifteenth century, it is possible to savour, more easily perhaps than anywhere else in Florence, the atmosphere of the early Renaissance and to imagine that we are living in the past. They are all fairly solemn, with the exception of the delightful *Young Lady with Flowers* (c.1480),

generally attributed to Verrocchio but in a pattern that plagues much of his finest work there are occasional suggestions that the real author is Leonardo da Vinci, his greatest pupil. It is set apart not just by its remarkable quality—the hands with their long, tapering fingers are particularly fine—but by its obviously sensual overtones. On the right of the entrance door stands a pair of rather stiff portraits of Cosimo il Vecchio's two sons by Mino da Fiesole, Ruskin's favourite Florentine sculptor. 'His chisel seems to cut life and carve breath, the marble burns beneath it, and becomes transparent with very spirit,' he wrote, and Pater called him the 'Raphael of sculpture', though it is now not easy to see why they felt his work was so incomparably superior to that of his contemporaries. Though most of these portraits are idealised and probably bear only a vague resemblance to their subjects, this is unlikely to be the case with the almost repellently realistic *Bust of Pietro Mellini* (1474) by Benedetto da Maiano with its great bulbous nose, warts and wrinkles like tram lines.

The two leading sculptors in Florence during

the second half of the fifteenth century were Antonio del Pollaiolo (1432–98) and Andrea del Verrocchio (1435–88). In the middle of the room are the two most famous works by both. Verrocchio was heavily influenced by Donatello and his *David* is clearly inspired by its famous forerunner, though it is anything but a copy. He uses the loose-fitting clothes to set in relief and heighten the tensely modelled, muscular body. It was made in 1473 for the Medici who for some reason, probably a shortage of cash, sold it to the Signoria three years later. Pollaiuolo's *Hercules and Antaeus* (c.1475), despite its small scale, has a remarkable power and energy based on his unrivalled powers of anatomical description that influenced many high Renaissance sculptors, including Michelangelo. Though condensing the power and movement of the male nude to a tiny scale, this is perfectly balanced around a central point of composition and is one of the first examples of Renaissance sculpture intended to be seen from multiple viewpoints.

The scores of bronze statuettes in Room 16 might be called the 'connoisseur's final frontier', for less is known about these figures than about any other field of Italian art. Mostly unsigned and undated, attributions have to be made solely on subjective visual judgement which allows endless scope for 'scholarly debate'. Small bronzes, like terracotta portrait busts, were first made in fifteenth-century Florence in a deliberate attempt to imitate the habits, ideas and works of art of the ancient Romans. Florence led the world in their manufacture until the end of the seventeenth century—long after her painters had become unimportant and provincial.

Room 17 contains a rather tawdry collection of armour and worth entering only to see Francesco da Sangallo's wonderfully emotive bust of Cosimo I's warrior father Giovanni delle Bande Nere which stands before the further window.

We cannot leave the Bargello without a visit to Room 1, which is on the ground floor and entered from the courtyard. It contains a fine collection of early sixteenth-century sculpture among which there are no less than four different works by Michelangelo. The *Drunken Bacchus* (1497) was made soon after he went to Rome for the first time.

It is a deliberate forgery of antique sculpture and Michelangelo is supposed to have smeared it with earth in order to make it look more genuinely antique before selling it to a collector. As an imitation of Roman sculpture it is all too successful—it has all the dull modelling and the inert, lifeless expression of Roman copies of Greek originals and if it were not by Michelangelo, I am tempted to think, it would probably be consigned to an obscure corner of the Uffizi, with a tag saying 'Roman. Second century A.D. Sculptor unknown'. Michelangelo's *Pitti Tondo* of the *Virgin and Child*, made in 1504, is similar to the *Taddei Tondo* in the Royal Academy, London, but in better condition. As in other half-completed examples of his work, the pleasure is to a great extent derived from a feeling, when looking in detail at the fine mesh of tiny chisel marks covering the surface, that we can picture Michelangelo himself working on the subject. The *Bust of Brutus* is one of the few of Michelangelo's works to which art historians attach a political significance. It was made shortly after one of the most horrendous episodes in Medicean history, the

murder of the unpleasant Duke Alessandro de' Medici by his half-brother Lorenzaccio in 1537, and makes an obvious symbolic reference to the virtues of tyrannicide.

At the far end of Room 1 are works by the generation of Florentine sculptors roughly contemporary with and heavily influenced by Michelangelo—that is Ammanati, Bandinelli and Cellini. Many of these are exquisite small-scale figures or groups. In old age Ammanati became deeply ashamed of his wonderfully erotic *Leda and the Swan* and began to produce work like his prim *Adam and Eve*. The range of Cellini's genius both as a master craftsman and as an innovative sculptor of stunning originality is apparent in his four bronze statuettes and the relief panel of *Perseus liberating Andromeda* (all made for the base of the Perseus in the Loggia dei Lanzi) and in the scenes that decorate the *Breastplate* of Cosimo I, the mean and pig-headed patron who largely ignored his talents. Though seldom given to modesty, Cellini remains strangely silent about this superb work in his famous autobiography. With its thin beard and weak mouth it perhaps provided an altogether too incisive character portrayal of a totalitarian ruler who wished to appear without mortal flaws. Cosimo himself seems to have preferred, to Cellini's shame, a blander portrayal by Bandinelli. The vitality of both makes a striking contrast with Giambologna's vast and dispassionate *Virtue Repressing Vice* (1570) and with Daniele da Volterra's dry *Bust of Michelangelo*, to the left before the door.

* * *

In Piazza S. Firenze there is a café where we might now be tempted to sit down and have a cup of coffee, but first we should look at **Palazzo Borghese** in Via Ghibellina, the street flanking the north side of the Bargello (No. 110). This is the most interesting example of neo-classical architecture in Florence and was built by one of the great 'survivors' of nineteenth-century Europe, the immensely rich Roman Prince Camillo Borghese. He married Napoleon's sister Pauline in 1803, became a Marshal of France and a governor of northern Italy, managed to survive Napoleon's fall and then turned to cultivating the Austrians with equal success. In fact this palazzo was built

(in 1822, by Gaetano Baccani) to give a party in honour of the Grand Duke of Tuscany, Ferdinand III, who was a first cousin of the Habsburg Emperor. It is worth a short detour to have a look into the vestibule, for it still retains most of its original trappings. There are two magnificent stone Egyptians just inside the main door, and along the pavement the original stone bollards still survive. Opposite, you may find it useful to note, is Florence's most expensive restaurant, the Enacoteca Pinchiorri.

But now for that coffee, and we could hope for few more delightful places to drink it. There is something curiously charming about this piazza. Behind us stands an unusually attractive palazzo, in front of us a magnificent example of the baroque, to the right a tremendous quoined angle clambers up the back of the Palazzo della Signoria, while to the north rise two towers, one octagonal, the other square, of the Badia and the Bargello. They all have interesting histories, particularly the baroque façade opposite, which was designed by two different architects and built in two quite separate stages. The left side is earlier than the rest of the building: it was completed in 1715 (and is the first important building by Ferdinando Ruggieri), was once free standing, and behind it there was and still is the church of S. Firenze Nuovo. The rest was added in the 1770s (by Zanobi del Rosso) who built a replica of Ruggieri's façade on the existing Romanesque church of S. Firenze and joined then together with an ingenious addition that looks appropriately monumental and gives the impression that it was all designed at the same time. This part of the building is now occupied by the Florentine law courts.

The history of **Palazzo Gondi** behind us is less complex, but then not quite as simple as it might seem. Though most of the façade is late fifteenth-century, by the most distinguished of Brunelleschi's followers, Giuliano da Sangallo, the last few metres of the left end as it reaches the corner and all of the façade up Via dei Gondi was added in the 1880s, though so tactfully that without a very close look it is not easy to tell.

And the towers? That to the right, of course, belongs to the Bargello, but that to the left? It belongs to the **Badia**, one of the oldest churches in Florence which, once we have finished our coffee and paid the bill, we must quickly visit. The tower is, in fact, the last reminder of the Badia's great age. It is eleventh-century and was built shortly after the foundation of the church. Everything else — the façade, the cloister and the interior — has, at different times, been altered. From the street we enter a fifteenth-century cloister. The interior is seventeenth-century and contains several fine Renaissance tombs, including Mino da Fiesole's *Monument to Count Ugo* (1469–81), a tenth-century benefactor of the Badia (a monastic foundation) whose reputation as a kindly man of peace is probably as firmly based on myth as that of the Good Duke Alfred in Norman Douglas' *South Wind*. Immediately to the left of the entrance is Filippino Lippi's large *Vision of St Bernard*. Above the right transept is a large beautiful grey lacquer and gilt organ and beneath it a baroque chapel with paintings by the seventeenth-century painter Francesco Furini and others. Devotees of Dante's *Divine Comedy* will be interested to know that it was here at the Badia, barely fifty years after the poet's death, that Boccaccio, already an old and sick man, gave his lectures on the great work.

Though it is possible to walk from here to S. Croce, one of the most famous of Florentine churches, in only five minutes, the streets between here and the basilica are so delightful and so full of 'sights' of interest that we are certain to become distracted and take at least five times as long. Taking the Borgo dei Greci (just to the right of the baroque building) we soon arrive in Via dei Bentaccordi, one of three curving streets which are built on the foundations of the Roman amphi-theatre and where some claim to be able to see signs of antique masonry on the lower storeys. Turning right, we can wander into the intriguing Piazza Peruzzi, one of the most romantic parts of old Florence, or by turning left, walking to the end of Via dei Bentaccordi and entering Vicolo delle Stinche we shall chance upon Vivoli, a café famous for its delicious fig and strawberry ice cream made by a family who, to judge from their healthy proportions, are clearly fond of it them-selves. Here the self-indulgent will be unable to resist a mid-morning *dolce* before, with ice cream in one hand and guide book in another, we make our way to Piazza S. Croce, where we might sit down on one of the stone benches at the near end and cast our gaze in the direction of the famous Franciscan basilica.

*   *   *

You need only look at Photograph **15** to see that Piazza S. Croce has undergone many changes in the last century. What E. M. Forster unkindly described as S. Croce's 'black and white façade of surpassing ugliness' was built in 1857–63 at the expense of Sir Francis Sloane, owner, I think, of that famous London Square. The façade is sup-posedly based on an original design by Andrea Orcagna, who Ruskin claimed was one of the three greatest Italian artists ever to have lived. This, however, can hardly be described as one of his most inspired designs, but it was an object of particular pride to both the English and the Italians in the latter half of the nineteenth cen-tury, though it is not generally admired today. The campanile is also nineteenth century. This was erected in the 1840s and opinions on its quality sharply differ. Murray's Guide of 1858, for instance, calls it 'a monument to bad taste and entirely out of keeping with the style of the church', while an authoritative writer on nineteenth-century Italian architecture in a more recent publication describes it as a 'clever and inventive design that passes to the eyes of most visitors to Florence for the genuine article'. We must decide for ourselves. The Piazza's other most interesting building, the fifteenth-century Palazzo Serristori-Cocchi, which stands behind us, facing the church, is something of a curiosity and seems wildly imaginative in comparison to most Florentine palazzi. On the right side there is the lovely Palazzo dell' Antella (No. 21) with a façade enlivened by fading frescoes of cavorting nymphs completed, according to a dubious story carried by every guide book, in only 21 days in 1619 by that superb and much-neglected seventeenth-century painter Giovanni da San Giovanni, doubtless with the help of a great many assistants. But lovely though the Piazza is, I cannot deny that there is something more than a little disappointing about its shops from which we must try to avert our attention. The colossal figure of a morose and

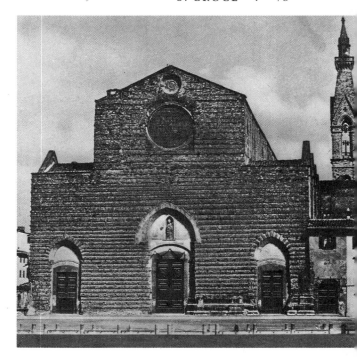

15

scowling Dante to the left of the façade (**16**) once had pride of place in the middle of the Piazza but has now mercifully been moved. The S. Croce quarter is the most densely populated in Florence, and it is also the lowest lying, which is why it suffered so badly in the flood of 1966. Oily, muddy water rose to almost 18 feet in the Piazza and sped around the streets at around 25 miles an hour, throwing cars against walls, destroying the interiors of shops, and ruining an estimated two million books in the Biblioteca Nazionale to the right of the basilica.

Now for the church. Despite its size—and it is the largest Franciscan basilica in Italy—the interior of S. Croce is remarkably cheerful. Light pours into the nave and across the white walls of the aisles, to which the burst of colour through the stained-glass windows of the choir makes a pleasant contrast. Though less dramatic than the soaring ecstasies of French Gothic there is an appealing, solid simplicity to S. Croce. The purpose of the building is at once clear: it was intended as a preaching hall for the vast congregations who came to hear the Franciscan sermons.

16

Its plain decoration and simple structure reflect Franciscan teaching and the life of the founder of the order, just as the subject of the paintings in the transept chapels and sacristy is dictated by the Franciscan idea that Christianity should be taught by a direct non-allegorical method that concentrates on the life of Christ and the saints.

S. Croce, as the Goncourts were not the first or the last to point out in the 1860s, is not simply a huge church and a vast gallery of fourteenth-century art but 'the Westminster Abbey of Italy'—a shrine to national genius containing the tombs of or monuments to some of the most famous Italian thinkers, writers and artists. It appealed particularly strongly to visitors to Florence in the early nineteenth century—like Mme de Staël for whom S. Croce was the most impressive of all the 'belles églises qui décorent cette ville', for it contained '. . . la plus brillante assemblée de morts qui soit peut-être en Europe', or Stendhal, who rushed here as soon as he arrived in Florence without even pausing to pay his respects to the Venus de' Medici.

On the entrance (west) wall stands a Monument to Gino Capponi (1), an earnest and distinguished nineteenth-century Tuscan politician who enjoyed telling his friends that the happiest years of his life had been spent in Scotland working as journalist on the *Edinburgh Review* which he acclaimed as 'the finest magazine ever published', a remark which may tell us as much about his character as about his taste in reading.

In the right-hand aisle Antonio Rossellino's charming *Madonna and Child* (2) (1478) faces Vasari's Tomb for Michelangelo (3) (1570) who agreed to be buried in Florence despite refusing to set foot in the city for the last 35 years of his life. Beside it is an enormous Monument to Dante (4)—monument we note, not tomb, since Dante died in exile and his remains lie in Ravenna. It seems ironic that the Florentines should have reserved their least distinguished monuments for their most distinguished writer. It was unveiled in 1829 (and is by the little known Stefano Ricci) when the sparkle had long gone out of neo-classicism. The Alfieri Monument (5) a little further on, completed twenty years earlier by Antonio Canova, the outstanding genius of neo-classical

Map 4
Plan of S. Croce

1. Monument to Gino Capponi
2. Rossellino's *Madonna and Child*
3. Tomb of Michelangelo
4. Monument to Dante
5. Monument to Alfieri
6. Pulpit by Benedetto da Maiano
7. Donatello's *Annunciation*
8. Tomb of Leonardo Bruni
9. Monument to Galileo
10. Monument to Machiavelli
11. Tomb of Carlo Marsuppini
12. Monument to Rossini
13. Monument to Vittorio Fossombroni
14. Portrait of Leon Battista Alberti
15. Bust of Princess Czartoryska
16. Tomb of Ugo Foscolo
17. Medici Chapel
18. Bardi Chapel
19. Peruzzi Chapel
20. Baroncelli Chapel
21. Castellani Chapel
22. Bardi di Libertà Chapel
23. Bardi di Vernio Chapel
24. Niccolini Chapel

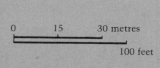

0   15   30 metres

100 feet

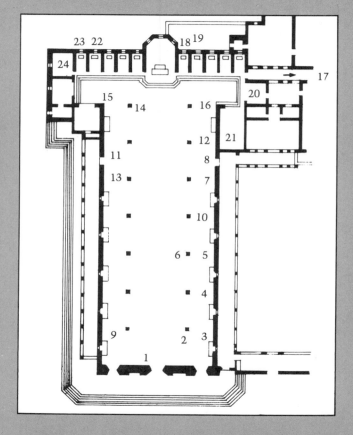

sculpture, is less academic and a great deal more subtle.

Passing on the left Benedetto da Maiano's marble pulpit (6) (1472–6) described by Edward Hutton as 'the finest Renaissance pulpit in all Italy' we continue up the aisle and encounter Donatello's *Annunciation* (7), one of his greatest works and once thought to be among his earliest but now considered a product of his maturity and dated between 1430 and 1440.

On the other side of the door stands Bernardo Rossellino's Tomb of Leonardo Bruni (8) (1444), an erudite fifteenth-century humanist and the first writer to draw a comparison between Florence and Athens. Born in Arezzo, he is usually called 'Aretino', which confused Mme de Staël into muddling him with Pietro Aretino, the friend of Titian and famous sixteenth-century caustic wit. 'Corinne', she says of the heroine of her great autobiographical novel, 'se sentit profondement émue en marchant entre ces deux rangées de tombeaux . . .' She sees a Monument to Galileo (9) to one side, a Monument to Machiavelli (10) to the other and then '. . . l'Arétin, cet homme qui a consacré ses jours à la plaisanterie et n'a rien éprouvé sur la terre de sérieux que la mort.' She could hardly have made a greater gaffe, as this Aretino led a most sober life and spent most of it translating Aristotle's *Ethics* and writing a *History of Florence*, the first major piece of Renaissance historical writing, which he holds in his hands.

This was to be the model of many other beautiful fifteenth-century tombs—most obviously of Desiderio da Settignano's perhaps even more lovely Tomb of Carlo Marsuppini (11) (1453) opposite (across the nave), and for the nineteenth-century Monument to Rossini (12) beside it. Though hailed at his death in 1868 as a 'composer of the Risorgimento' and given a much-prized post amongst his Italian forebears, Rossini wrote almost nothing after the *William Tell Overture* in 1828 and spent most of his life in Paris where he was famous for an idleness not entirely in the spirit of the Risorgimento.

Returning to the back of the nave we come to a monument to the great scientist and perhaps the last really great Tuscan—Galileo Galilei (9) (1564–1642) by Foggini (1737). Tried by the

Inquisition for his belief that the earth was not the centre of the universe, Galileo was forced to retract and spent his last twenty years as a virtual prisoner in a villa at Arcetri. Though it speaks in favour of the Medicean Grand Dukes that they afforded Galileo at least some protection against the Inquisition, he was not permitted a Christian burial inside the church until the death of Gian Gastone in 1737.

To the left of the door in the north aisle is a Monument to Leonardo Fossombroni (13) who was Prime Minister of Tuscany for much of the first half of the nineteenth century. Rather wittier if less famous than his contemporary Gino Capponi, he was well known for his ironic *bons mots*. Once, when a secretary spilled a bottle of ink over some important state papers which had just received his signature and exclaimed in alarm 'What now?' he replied in a voice of absolute calm 'Now, my dear fellow? Now let us go and have dinner.' 'But the business,' the secretary replied. 'Tomorrow, my dear fellow, tomorrow. Dinner will burn, the state will not.'

Though Alberti no doubt said many things wit-tier and more ironic, history does not record what they were, and though there are many good reasons for reading his works on artistic and archi-tectural theory, it is not for amusement. He looks faintly absurd in his idealised portrait by Lorenzo Bartolini (14) on the last pillar to the left. Less pompous and studied, Bartolini's bust of the Rus-sian Princess Czartoryska (15) in the left transept is the most ingratiating and likeable example of nineteenth-century sculpture in Florence. Finally there is the tomb of Ugo Foscolo (16) who, born in the Ionian Islands in 1778, is an exact counterpart to Byron, and like him realised all the passions of the Napoleonic age. He served in Napoleon's army, then after 1814 sought refuge in London and was lionised by the Holland House set, but ultimately died a pauper in 1827 and was buried at Turnham Green. One of the first acts of unified Italy was to claim the body of the poet patriot and it was translated to S. Croce in 1871. His poetry, though occasionally rather heavy on classical allu-sion, is remarkably beautiful, and there can be nowhere more appropriate than S. Croce to read his macabre masterpiece '*Dei Sepolcri*' in which the living collaborate with the dead and the Past is made to live in the Present.

In the Cappella Medici (17), the long, thin room at the end of the corridor beyond the south transept, there hangs a superb della Robbia altarpiece and, to its right, a relief of the *Madonna and Child* (to the right of the altar) which has an intriguing history. It is a nineteenth-century forgery in the style of the early Renaissance, which for a long time was accepted by all the greatest scholars as the work of Donatello. It was left to S. Croce, perhaps in a deliberate attempt to humiliate connoisseurs of sculpture, by a shady Lucchese art dealer called Francesco Lombardi in 1868 and the forgery only came to light in the early years of this century.

So much for the tombs and monuments, now turn your attention to S. Croce's paintings and begin with the Bardi (18) and Peruzzi (19) Chapels (the first two chapels to the right of the choir), containing the most important frescoes outside the Arena Chapel in Padua by the greatest Italian artist of the later Middle Ages, Giotto di Bondone (1266/7–1337).

Though later than Giotto's frescoes in the Arena Chapel at Padua, through a mixture of human and natural causes these survive in a much worse condition. Perhaps because he was already an elderly man when he undertook the commission they were mainly painted 'a secco' onto dry plaster rather than in the more demanding but much more durable technique of 'true' fresco which entails applying the pigment to the plaster while it is still damp and fresh (thus *fresco*). Then in the early eighteenth century, at the nadir of Giotto's reputation, both chapels were redecorated and their frescoes whitewashed over only to be rediscovered in the mid-nineteenth century and 'restored', which at the time meant repainted. In the 1960s the repainting was removed, revealing what was by then left of Giotto's original.

Though the result is disconcerting at first sight, for there are large patches of bare plaster between the surviving frescoes, enough remains to make them of more than academic interest. Some of the *Scenes from the Life of St Francis* in the chapel on the left, the Bardi Chapel (c.1315–20), or the *Scenes from the Life of St John the Divine* (right wall) and *St John the Baptist* (left wall) in the Peruzzi Chapel (c.1326–30) convey Giotto's legendary ability to get straight to the heart of whatever biblical story he represents. The number of figures and their actions are cut down to the bare minimum, thus conveying highly complex stories in the clearest possible way.

Through the course of the fourteenth century most of the chapels in S. Croce were painted by Giotto's followers and pupils. The most interesting and important are Taddeo Gaddi's *Scenes from the Life of the Virgin* in the Baroncelli Chapel (20) (1332–8) and his son Agnolo Gaddi's (about whom nothing is known other than that he was once fined for beating up a tax collector) paintings around the choir, *The Legend of the True Cross* (c.1375) and in the Castellani Chapel (21), *Scenes from the Lives of Saints* (c.1385). Those who are seriously interested in trecento art, however, will not miss the Bardi di Libertà Chapel (22) and beside it, furthest from the choir, the Bardi di Vernio Chapel (23) containing frescoes respectively by Bernardo Daddi and Maso di Banco. The latter are particularly interesting for their experimental developments of Giotto's style. Those who find it difficult to respond to early Tuscan art can console themselves by looking instead at the most extravagant and successful example of baroque decoration in Florence, the Niccolini Chapel (24). A fantasy of green and brown marbles, it was designed by the comparatively unknown Antonio Dossi and built from 1579 to 1584. The paintings are by Alessandro Allori and the sculpture by Francavilla. The persistent have been known to persuade the sacristan to open it. Before leaving the church we should not forget to look into the chapel to its left (the central chapel of the left transept) which contains a famous Crucifix by Donatello that Brunelleschi is supposed to have criticised as resembling a 'peasant on the cross'.

Leaving S. Croce, turn immediately left and you come to the entrance to the cloisters (entrance ticket; for opening times, see p. 231). At the far end of the first cloister stands a small building universally recognised as one of the outstanding achievements of the early Renaissance—the Pazzi Chapel by Brunelleschi. A combination and evocation of what many see as the most important aspects of the early Renaissance, it is an essay in perfect proportional balance and the quintessence of what has been called the 'architecture of humanism'. In recent years, however, the attribution of the design of the Pazzi Chapel, or at least of its façade, has become something of an academic *cause célèbre*. The chapel was begun in c.1443, though the façade was not completed until the 1480s—more than twenty years after Brunelleschi's death. This has led some architectural historians to suggest that the façade may have been designed by Benedetto da Maiano who supervised the project from c.1460.

The interior is the coldest and purest of Brunelleschi's buildings. It is entirely composed of perfect forms—a hemispherical dome, for instance, rises from a square drum flanked by half cubes. The decoration of the walls, with their grey pietra serena pilasters and their Luca della Robbia Apostles in tondos, and of the floor, is reduced to a bare minimum and calculated to emphasise the proportional scheme.

To the right of the first cloister is the S. Croce Museum. By the entrance, now prudently attached to a pulley, is the famous Cimabue *Crucifix* virtually destroyed in the flood of 1966. If Giotto's frescoes in the basilica are the corpse of a great work of art this is no more than the bleached bones of a skeleton, despite a masterly if highly controversial restoration in which the damaged areas have not been entirely repainted. On the wall opposite is Donatello's gilded bronze *St Louis* (1423), made for Or San Michele, which he considered to be one of his least successful works. On the far wall is the *Last Supper* by Taddeo Gaddi and assistants. The remaining rooms of the museum contain nothing of very great interest.

The second cloister of S. Croce, possibly designed by Brunelleschi though it was built after his death, is almost oriental in its extreme sophistication and delicacy. Its magic survived a near submersion in 1966 by the waters of the flood. (**17**)

* * *

If you walk up Borgo S. Croce (which runs at an angle to the left of the façade of the basilica) leading to Via de' Benci, you arrive immediately

outside the entrance to the **Fondazione Horne** (Via dei Benci 6, opening times, see p. 230) a small but rich collection left to the city of Florence on his death in 1916 by Herbert Percy Horne (1844–1916), a reclusive and scholarly art historian who has been described as 'the most distinguished Englishman not to appear in the *Dictionary of National Biography*'. He managed to assemble a very fine collection with limited resources. The entire contents of his palazzo probably cost less than the sums spent by the 'squillionaires' collecting at the same time—Pierpont Morgan, Arnhelm and others—on a single picture. Haunting the Florentine dealers, he claimed that a shrewd collector could buy originals of fourteenth- and fifteenth-century Italian art for less than the price of reproductions. The greatest achievement of his life was not, despite its charm and quality, this collection but his monograph on Botticelli which appeared in 1911 and is still perhaps the greatest artistic monograph in the English language.

A steep staircase leads to the first floor. There are catalogues in every room listing dates and the names of artists. Of particular quality in Room I on the first floor are the pictures on the far wall among which there is an altarpiece of three saints by the fourteenth-century Sienese artist Pietro Lorenzetti. Immediately below is a tondo of the *Madonna and Child*, an uncharacteristically conventional painting by Piero di Cosimo (1462–1521), an eccentric and puzzling Florentine artist who spans the fifteenth and sixteenth centuries. According to Vasari he lived on hard-boiled eggs cooked in home-made glue. The small, majestic religious paintings on the table to the right by Bernardo Daddi and Simone Martini, both Sienese artists, were probably used in the home and brought out on important religious festivals. In Room II are two paintings by the seventeenth-century artist Francesco Furini who, unlike his contemporaries, painted erotic subjects and went on doing so after he became a priest at the age of 42, and *St Stephen* by Giotto, arguably Horne's best picture. On the second floor is an interesting collection of fourteenth- to sixteenth-century domestic utensils and in the smaller room to the right some fine fourteenth-century furniture.

We emerge from Horne's palazzo back into Via

de' Benci and must decide where to have lunch. There is no shortage of good and cheap restaurants in S. Croce. A little way up Via de' Benci (which changes its name to Via Verdi at the other side of Piazza S. Croce) is La Maremma da Giuliano or at 47 Corso dei Tintori (which runs past the left façade of the palazzo to the Biblioteca Nazionale between S. Croce and the river) is Il Fagiolo, and there are others just as good not much further away. Alternatively we could wait for Bus No. 13 which stops beside the palazzo and will take us up to Piazzale Michelangelo and the rather more glamorous La Loggia, which has a fine view over the city and is as good a place as any to digest the impressions gained from a hurried visit to some of Florence's greatest treasures.

4

THE UFFIZI

✤ The Galleria degli Uffizi (opening times, see p. 231) running from the Piazza della Signoria to the Lungarno contains one of the greatest art collections in Europe.

The palazzo was first used as a public art gallery in the eighteenth century and ever since then its reputation as one of the most challenging and exacting cultural assault courses in Europe has been growing steadily. Lady Blessington, friend of Byron and author of *An Idler in Italy*, who thought but little of scaling Alpine passes or climbing Vesuvius, had to admit after her first day in the Uffizi that 'there are few pleasures more fatiguing than viewing an extensive gallery of fine arts'. Less stalwart visitors, like Wordsworth who grew so weary that he fell asleep in a chair provided by a kindly museum official, have collapsed before they reached the last rooms, and in 1938 Mussolini, perspiring heavily while following an enthusiastic Hitler who insisted on seeing every one of its 1700 paintings, was heard to mutter 'all these damn pictures' long before he reached the exit. Many others have doubtless felt the same way even if they have not said so, and have found that by the time they re-emerge from the Uffizi they can scarcely stagger to the Café Rivoire in Piazza della Signoria to refresh themselves with Campari and coffee. In order to avoid the same fate visitors are advised not to attempt to see the entire collection on a single visit!

Begin by looking at the building itself, which like many other great galleries was never intended to be one. Designed by Giorgio Vasari (who is more famous as the author of his famous *Lives of the Artists* than as an architect), it was begun by Cosimo I in 1560 and intended to be the most impressive state secretariat in sixteenth-century Italy. Like the buildings to which it is best compared—the Capitol in Rome or Sansovino's library in the Piazza S. Marco, Venice—it is meant to be eye-catchingly extravagant and ostentatious, a symbol of the power of the state and the wealth and prestige of its ruler. It looks its best from the arcade that fronts the river. From here, looking up the long Piazza that leads into the Signoria it looks wonderfully, almost theatrically grand. (18) But fine as it is, there can be no denying that the Uffizi is a little joyless. Despite a brave attempt to cheer it up by a director of the gallery in the middle of the last century who filled the then empty niches along its façades with new life-size statues of figures from the Florentine Renaissance, it con-

tinues to remain a sombre building.

After buying tickets you are faced with the decision of whether or not to take the lift up to the galleries, which are on the top floor. Before making a final decision you should remember the words of a character in a novel by Ronald Firbank who declares that 'middle age begins when you take in the lift in the Uffizi'. While the stairs are incomparably more exciting, the lift is undeniably more restful and contains an interesting if depressing little graph, constantly updated by the dynamic museum staff, which tells you that the annual number of visitors to the Uffizi has increased from 100,000 to 1.6 million in the last 25 years. As you proceed through the gallery you may not find these statistics difficult to believe. If it is March or April you may wish that many of the statistics had stayed at school.

At the top of the stairs there are busts of all the Medicean Grand Dukes. Generations of visitors have taken pleasure in observing the decline in their physical features from a Machiavellian masculinity in the sixteenth century to the bloated, bewigged, heavy jawed and ripe-lipped *fin*

18

de race Gian Gastone who looks like some gruesome caricature of Louis XIV in his less handsome
years. Walk straight through the room beyond
them and you find yourself in the great corridor
that much impressed Henry James when he first
came here in the 1870s.

The statues that line either side of the corridor
are mostly Roman. Until about 1860 these and
other, even finer, pieces in the gallery, were considered to be the greatest jewels of the Medicean
collection. In fact during the eighteenth and
nineteenth centuries the chief attraction of
Florence to the rest of the world was that it
contained the best, and until the excavation of
Herculaneum the only, large public collection of
antique sculpture outside Rome. So when Goethe,
William Beckford, Byron or Americans like James
Fenimore Cooper or Nathaniel Hawthorne came
to the Uffizi it was not primarily to look at Correg-
gios and Carraccis or Lippis and Leonardos but to
rhapsodise over Venuses or the busts of Senators
and Emperors, sigh at the agony of Dying Gladi-
ators, marvel at the lithe energy of Dancing Fauns
and the shattered pieces of antique torso and limb
that we now see in such profusion around us. The
awe in which such objects were held is never more
apparent than when you read the notes taken by
Percy Bysshe Shelley in his many visits to the
gallery in the spring of 1817. Incredibly enough,
among all the pages and pages of impressions and
hyperbole he never so much as mentions a
painting!

These marbles were not, of course, found in
Tuscany. Almost without exception they were
excavated in Rome between the sixteenth and
eighteenth centuries and diligently collected first
by the Medici Popes and then by every Grand
Duke and kept at the Villa Medici in Rome. From
about 1600 they were gradually brought to
Florence, and the Uffizi became a gallery to
accommodate them.

The second half of the nineteenth century saw a
revolution in popular taste that was to leave the
antique marbles virtually neglected and focus
attention on early Italian art. Though it now
seems incredible, the early Tuscan religious paintings that now cover the walls of Rooms 2 to 4,
were, until at least the middle of the nineteenth

century, generally valued more for the gold in their backgrounds than as works of art, and there are several well-known cases of their being melted down in order to extract the metal. Countless early paintings, thought to be of little aesthetic or material value, were simply thrown out of houses and churches. Robert Browning, living in Florence in the late 1840s and the 1850s, found beautiful fourteenth-century altarpieces in junk shops, lying under piles of dust and old books. The famous collection of early Italian art now at Yale was purchased in Florence for very small sums at roughly the same time.

All that had changed by the 1870s. Ruskin's *Mornings in Florence* begins with the words, 'If there be one artist, more than another, whose work it is desirable that you see in Florence . . . it is Giotto.' By the end of the century fashion had turned its full circle as art historians published endless unreadable monographs, full of earnest discussion on the importance of texture and functional line, about the most minor and obscure painters with names like Mariotto di Nardo and Cola di Petrucciola whose works, to mere amateurs, seem to look alarmingly similar.

The three wonderful altarpieces of the *Maestà* (*Madonna and Child in Majesty*) in Room 2 sweep the visitor straight into the great age of Italian piety. They were painted during the late thirteenth and early fourteenth centuries when the whole of central Italy experienced a remarkable bout of religious energy and Florence built its two great basilicas of S. Croce and S. Maria Novella. These Madonnas are by the best known and most successful painters of the age— Cimabue (late thirteenth century, whose name is thought by some to be no more than a convenient term applied by scholars to a collection of works of art in a similar style) and Giotto (1266/7–1337) who were both Florentines, and Duccio di Buoninsegna (died 1318 or '19), who was Sienese. It is hard to imagine these paintings as they were intended to be seen, that is in the apse of a dark church or in a family chapel surrounded by candles whose flickering light just picks out the threads of silver and gold in the Madonna's cloak and the angels' wings, the lines of the throne and the face of the child Christ. Though they give pleasure to us as aesthetic objects, to a late medieval Tuscan these were objects of mysterious power and a link with the Divine. To fully appreciate them this must be understood.

Vasari in his *Lives of the Artists* holds these three artists, and Giotto in particular, as being responsible for the rebirth of Western painting after many centuries during which it had merely imitated the two-dimensional style of Byzantine art. While this is a gross simplification, even the briefest look at these paintings illustrates the rapid development of artistic style in Tuscany from c.1280–1310. The differences between the Cimabue and the Duccio, both painted between 1280 and 1290, are less marked than between these two paintings and the Giotto of 1310. Nevertheless there are clear developments in the artists' ability to create a convincing representation of objects in three dimensions. While in the Cimabue it is impossible to tell, for example, whether the central arch of the throne recedes or rises, the same cannot be said of the Duccio, which imparts a sense of recession and depth in a more sophisticated way.

The comparative lack of interest shown in perspective by both artists, however, is illustrated not only by the prophets at the base of the throne who are on a smaller scale than the other figures, but also by the angels which appear to hang unrealistically in mid-air to either side of the Madonna. In the Giotto *Maestà*, painted in 1310 for Ognissanti, this is not the case. Here the prophets are on the same scale as the other figures and the angels stand firmly on the ground twisting their heads in different directions. The Madonna sits comfortably on a throne that has been constructed by the use of simple rules of perspective and placed on a stepped dais.

All three artists have been subject to a dose of weighty monographs. Berenson's description of the magic of Giotto, working a limited vocabulary to death, became a joke almost as soon as it was written. Here is an extract: '. . . every time our eyes recognise reality we are, as a matter of fact, giving tactile values to retinal impressions . . . the essential in the art of painting . . . is somehow to stimulate our consciousness of tactile values . . . to realise form we must give tactile values to retinal sensations . . .' And so it continues for yet another lengthy paragraph.

The next two rooms are filled with fourteenth-century paintings from Tuscan churches—the greatest of them, by Simone Martini and the Lorenzetti, are Sienese. Rooms 5 and 6 are one room filled with early high Gothic art of the fifteenth century. On the right wall is the *Adoration of the Magi* (1423) by Gentile da Fabriano—arguably the greatest single masterpiece associated with the International Gothic style in Italy. It was painted, though this is difficult to believe, only two or three years before Masaccio's frescoes in the Brancacci Chapel. It is a work of consummate beauty. The cavalcade, the countryside, the animals, the clothes, even the sky is painted with a love of the purely decorative and a sure feeling for colour that combine to make this one of the most lovely paintings in the gallery.

If you detest high Gothic art or share Aldous Huxley's aversion to what he called 'acres of Christmas card primitives' then take the door to the right of Giotto's *Maestà* that leads into Room 7, which in a step allows you to bypass nearly one and a half centuries of Italian art.

Room 7 takes you from Gothic to Renaissance. Most of these paintings date from between 1430 and 1460, one of the most productive and interesting phases of Florentine art. The earliest are minor works by great masters—Masaccio and Masolino's *Virgin and Child with St Anne* (c.1424, the Virgin and the Child are by Masaccio) and Fra Angelico's *Coronation of the Virgin* (c.1430). More interesting are the slightly later paintings by artists who, in different ways, digested the breakthroughs of the early Renaissance titans. Paolo Uccello's fabulous *Rout of S. Romano* (c.1456) which once hung in the bedroom of Lorenzo the Magnificent in the Palazzo Medici-Riccardi perhaps gives us less pleasure than it must have given him since its two flanking panels were sold to the National Gallery in London and the Louvre in the nineteenth century.

The *St Lucy Altarpiece* (1445–8), opposite, by Domenico Veneziano (died 1461) is one of the first paintings to put the Madonna and Saints in a single unified scene, instead of dividing them into panels as in a Gothic polyptych. Domenico's paintings are as lovely as they are rare—there are only a dozen surviving examples of his work. One of the only things known for certain about his life is that he died penniless in a Florentine work-house, so it can safely be assumed that his serene architectural backgrounds, his pale pinks and greens and his calm, saintly faces were less pleasing to the patrons of Renaissance Florence than they are to us.

Beside the window is a double-sided double portrait by the fifteenth-century artist now perhaps more admired than any other—Piero della Francesca (1416–92). He was a surprisingly late discovery. Long after his contemporaries' work was well known he remained obscure—partly because his paintings in his home town of Borgo S. Sepolcro, in Urbino, and in Arezzo, are off the beaten track. These two portraits are not of Cosimo il Vecchio but of a very different and in some ways more extraordinary patron and his wife—Federigo da Montefeltro, Duke of Urbino, who embellished his state and built his exquisite Palazzo Ducale by hiring himself out as a condot-tiere. This has all the sparkling, radiant light, the fine, precise detail and the combination of sophistication with simplicity that characterises all of Piero's work. The reverse sides take you even further from reality and into a clear-aired, still and timeless world of allegory. The Duke and Duchess, on different panels, ride towards each other on chariots pulled by unicorns, their directions guided by angels and accompanied by appropriate male and female virtues, in front of a landscape that you think must be a creation of the imagination until you go to visit the countryside around Borgo S. Sepolcro and see that it is not.

Room 8 is full of paintings by the fifteenth century's most refreshingly bohemian if embarrassingly amorous genius—Fra Filippo Lippi. Vasari's descriptions of his romantic escapades and his abduction and seduction of a not so demure nun contribute the most amusing and readable pages to the *Lives of the Artists*. Between sin and seduction he somehow found time to paint these enchanting pure, lovely Madonnas. Slowly, as we move around the room they become more delicate and a little lovelier until we arrive at his most poetic *Madonna and Child* with Angels set in a landscape that clearly influenced Leonardo.

Room 9 need only delay you because it contains two small paintings of the *Labours of Hercules* by an artist much patronised by Lorenzo the Magnificent, Antonio Pollaiuolo (1433–98) who should not be confused with his more pedestrian brother Piero, whose paintings are also in this room. Antonio carried out the first recorded dissections of the human body of the Renaissance in an attempt to comprehend the anatomical structure of man. Though a sculptor of great talent he was above all a draughtsman of genius, next to Leonardo perhaps the greatest of the fifteenth century. These paintings, notwithstanding their small scale, convey the swelling, twisting power of muscled limbs and exploit the full potential of the single line.

Immediately to your left as you come into the large room beyond is a small picture, gallantly labelled by the gallery as a self-portrait by Filippino Lippi, thought by many to be a clever forgery. It mysteriously appeared in the collection of Ignazio Hugford, one of the shadier if more talented members of the English community in Florence in the eighteenth century, who sold it to the Grand Dukes. Hugford, like his more famous friend Thomas Patch, was a dealer and a connoisseur as well as a painter, and this is just one of several forgeries of which he is suspected.

Rooms 10–14 were knocked into one in the early 1970s to contain the crowds of eager art lovers who gather beneath the charming and mysterious mythological paintings by Sandro Botticelli (c.1445–1510), one of the greatest Florentine artists. Though these are now perhaps the best known paintings of the Florentine Renaissance they were not publicly displayed until 1815 and in England went virtually unnoticed until the last quarter of the nineteenth century. The first Englishman to write about them seriously was Swinburne in 1868. By 1880, when *Punch* published the famous cartoon of two men in conversation, one asking 'Do you like Botticelli?' and the other replying, 'No, I prefer Chianti,' the 'Botticelli boom' had taken off.

A large proportion of the avalanche of words written about Botticelli since then has been devoted to unravelling the very complex allegori-

cal subtleties of the *Primavera*. It was commissioned for a second cousin of Lorenzo the Magnificent called Lorenzo di Pierfrancesco de' Medici,
who cannot have been more than fifteen years old
when it was painted, probably as an inexpensive
substitute for tapestry which, contrary to modern
values, was more prestigious than painting and
about ten times more expensive per square foot.
The complex allegory that forms its subject was
probably devised by Marsilio Ficino or Poliziano,
two important figures in the intellectual circle
that revolved around the Medici.

Today art historians tend to play down the more
bizarre explanations of the *Primavera*. Although
there is still no general agreement on its subject
and meaning, most scholars seem to believe that it
can be 'read' from right to left as an allegory of the
trials of love. To the far right the wind god *Zephyr*
touches the nymph *Chloris* who becomes *Flora*,
goddess of spring (with flowers pouring out of her
mouth), representing love in its most idyllic form.
Venus stands in the centre with a coy expression
that seems to warn that love is something more
complicated and dangerous. To her left the three
Graces, each symbolising one of the many facets
of love, dance in a circle. *Cupid*, blindfolded
above, irresponsibly shoots off arrows without the
faintest idea of where they may land, while
Mercury, to the far left, has his back turned to the
entire scene, emphasising the fickleness of men.
That, at least, is one possible explanation.

Botticelli probably began his career in the studio
of Filippo Lippi. During the 1470s and the early
1480s he enjoyed the patronage of the Medici. One
of his earliest paintings in this room, *The Adoration of the Magi* (c.1475, left wall), includes
several of the Medici among the spectators. He
reached the height of his success in early middle
age with the mythological paintings but soon
afterwards, after the expulsion of the Medici from
Florence in 1494, seems to have become less
fashionable and his paintings become more linear
and neurotic. An equivalent transformation is also
visible in the work of some contemporaries and is
generally attributed both to the changing atmosphere in Florence after the fall of the Medici, the
rise of Savonarola and to the influence of northern
European art which first arrives in Florence with

the *Portinari Altarpiece* by Hugo van der Goes (standing at the centre of the room), which was commissioned by the agent of the Medici bank in Antwerp and arrived in Florence in 1480.

Room 15 contains the early work of the most wide ranging and fascinating genius in the history of Western culture—Leonardo da Vinci (1452–1519). Born the illegitimate son of a notary in Vinci, near Pisa, Leonardo began his career in the studio of Andrea del Verrocchio. His earliest known work, executed when he was less than twenty years old, is the angel in Verrocchio's *Baptism* (1470, right wall). He is almost certainly responsible for a much larger part of the *Annunciation* (c.1475) though just how much of this painting is by Leonardo and how much by Verrocchio or by Lorenzo di Credi is much contested.

On the facing wall is a large, unfinished *Adoration of the Magi* (1481–2) on which Leonardo spent seven months before leaving Florence to accept an offer from Lodovico Sforza to join his court in Milan as an engineer/artist extraordinary, willing to turn his hand to any problem from building dams on the Po to installing central heating in the Duke's private apartments. Though unfinished it has been called the first painting of the high Renaissance. In comparison to the work of his contemporaries, most conveniently with the *Annunciation* by Lorenzo di Credi which hangs on the left wall, it seems wildly experimental and energetic.

When he departed for Milan Leonardo had only just begun to put on the underpaint. Though at first it seems a confused tangle of charcoaled lines, the longer one looks at it the clearer and more intriguing it becomes—figures are superimposed on top of one another in a chaos that suggests infinite possibilities. The figures are arranged, though this is not immediately clear, in a simple composition uniting a semi-circle with a pyramid that was to be copied and recopied by artists all over Italy during the next century.

By this stage the Uffizi's heavily didactic arrangement, where the paintings are arranged in strict chronological order so as to emphasise the influence of one generation and of one painter on another, can begin to feel a little like a lavishly illustrated textbook on the history of Italian art.

But now we come to a welcome interruption in the chronological sequence as we reach the Tribuna (Room 18, entered from the corridor), which was the first room in the Uffizi to be used as a gallery. It was decorated by Buontalenti, a brilliantly inventive court architect who specialised in the creation of just this kind of small-scale, semi-theatrical splendour, for Francesco I in the 1580s as a showplace for his most treasured possessions. The ceiling, encrusted with mother-of-pearl, is particularly remarkable and typical of Buontalenti's imaginative flair. It still preserves some of the feeling of disorganised romantic clutter and opulent, ordered chaos caught and exaggerated by Johann Zoffany in his painting of the Tribuna (**19**) commissioned by the English Royal Family.

Zoffany paints the Tribuna jammed full not just of paintings and sculpture but of people—the leading members of the English community in Florence in the 1760s. The figure standing to the right wearing a conspicuous star on his coat and a sword is Sir Horace Mann, English envoy to Tuscany for almost forty years. As famous for his good manners as for his gross snobbery, he would sometimes accompany the more important young grand tourists to the Tribuna in the evenings, where they would enjoy a little conversation with Signor Bianchi (a museum official who offended them all very much when he robbed the gallery and then set it on fire in 1763), before turning with affection towards the *Medici Venus* standing at the centre of the room, a work of art that demonstrates perhaps better than any other the amusing vicissitudes of the history of taste.

It arrived in Florence in 1677 and in a short time became one of the most celebrated and universally admired pieces of antique sculpture. Though now regarded as a fine but not exceptional and imperfectly restored (the tilt of the head, for instance, results from inept restoration) example of Greek sculpture dating from about 200 B.C., from the early eighteenth to the late nineteenth century it commanded a reputation only comparable to that of the Sistine ceiling or the *Mona Lisa* today. During that time, with very few exceptions, the travel journals of English, American, French and German tourists, scholars and connoisseurs contain an embarrassing eulogy of its qualities. For

19

the hyper-intelligent German scholar Winckelmann she represented '. . . a rose which after a lovely dawn unfolds its leaves to the rising sun; resembles one who is passing from one age which is hard and somewhat harsh—like fruits before their perfect ripeness—into another . . .' Byron, usually so damning about art, who thought the Parthenon '. . . rather like the Mansion House' and S. Croce '. . . much illustrious nothing' wrote five stanzas of *Childe Harold* in an attempt, as he says in his concluding line, 'to describe the indescribable' before retiring, 'drunk with beauty'. Even Ruskin fell into the trap. On his first visit in 1840 he wrote 'the Venus, usually in her casts a foolish little schoolgirl, is one of the purest and most elevated incarnations of Woman conceivable', though in his autobiography written in old age he was to claim that, at first sight he had '. . . at once proclaimed . . . the Medici Venus an uninteresting little person.'

Napoleon took the Venus de' Medici back to Paris in 1802 but only after a struggle, as the Florentines took the precaution of despatching her and other important objects in the gallery to Palermo before his agents arrived. Just about the only people who did not admire the Venus de' Medici were those nineteenth-century prigs who found nudity offensive, such as the Scottish Presbyterian Reverend Muckleman in a novel by Charlotte Eaton who, when he turns into the Tribuna simply exclaims 'Gude Lord, she's stark naked!' and hastily backs from the room.

Not all of the antique sculpture in the Uffizi has experienced such a dramatic fall in reputation. The *Dancing Faun* and *The Wrestlers*, both in this room, are still generally considered some of the finest pieces of sculpture to survive from antiquity.

Ironically what now seizes the attention of many visitors to the Tribuna are the portraits by Agnolo Bronzino (1503–72), an artist who evokes a world that admirers of the Venus de' Medici probably deplored and condemned. The piercing eyes, malevolent half smiles and the fine, brilliantly coloured clothes of his sitters take one closer than anything else to the sophisticated, urbane, highly educated yet cruel world of sixteenth-century Italy and are in the most complete sense an evocation of the Medicean court at the time of Cosimo I.

The door to the right of the Tribuna leads into three smallish and agreeable rooms. In the second, Room 20, is Dürer's *Portrait of his Father* and in the third is the famous *Sacred Allegory* by the Venetian Giovanni Bellini. But as few of the pictures are by a Florentine we have a convenient excuse to delay seeing them until another day and can instead refresh our minds either by enjoying the views from the windows at the end of the corridor or by walking to the gallery café at the far end of the west corridor.

In Room 25 (the first room in the west corridor) is the *Doni Tondo* by Michelangelo (1503) which, though it was awarded only one star out of a possible five for artistic merit by an English guide book in the last century, is arguably the most important painting of the early sixteenth century in Florence. He worked on it at the same time as on the *David*, at that magic moment when the other great high Renaissance figures, Raphael and Leonardo, were also in Florence. As the only painting by Michelangelo outside Rome it provided the most important influence for the next generation of Florentine painters — that is for the Mannerists exhibited in this and the next two rooms

The effect of the *Doni Tondo* derives partly from its composition. You look at the Madonna from an unusually low position, so she appears to advance from the frame. Her curious spiralling movement gives the painting its central focus as well as in itself implying a sphere. Equally unusual are the curious naked male figures, possibly angels, in the background. But it was not so much the composition as Michelangelo's technique of rendering the body that influenced his Florentine contemporaries and the younger generation. The arms and legs of the Madonna have a sculptured, polished quality and the faces of the figures have modelled and hollow cheekbones rather as if they were made of stone. The deliberately shocking, unusual colours and his use of bright surface glazes were to make a dramatic contribution to the art of the next generation.

The first important Florentine Mannerist was Rosso Fiorentino, whose *Moses Defending the Children of Jethro* (1524), also in Room 25, has a wild violence that is deliberately intended to shock. On every wall of Rooms 26 and 27 there are ravishing paintings, amongst which the loveliest is Raphael's *Madonna del Cardellino* but they will probably have to wait until your next visit if you are not to go the same way as Wordsworth and Mussolini. Ignore, on this occasion, the demanding *angst* of Florentine mannerism and walk on to Room 28 which is full of paintings much more likely to suit your mood. You find yourself standing in the very different world evoked by the greatest Venetian painter—Titian (1485–1576). To some extent isolated, geographically and psychologically, from the political upheavals and stylistic innovations of the rest of Italy, showered with commissions from every monarch and prince in Europe, he painted pictures glorifying, without the smallest trace of a guilty social or spiritual conscience, the life and wealth of the Venetian aristocracy. None of these paintings appears to have the intellectual preoccupations so obvious in the work of his Florentine contemporaries. The *Venus of Urbino* (1538) is one of the most overtly and deliciously erotic nudes ever painted and invites a long, pleasurable and relaxed admiration.

In the opulent piano nobile of a palazzo that forms the setting you can almost imagine the Venetians whose portraits hang on the opposite wall gathered for a ball.

In Room 29 is the masterpiece of perhaps the most technically accomplished of the Mannerists, Parmigianino (1503–40). *The Madonna del Collo Lungo* (1534–40) is one of the most ostentatiously clever of all his paintings, and takes us into that half real, half fantastic world where art demands that we suspend belief. The angels to the left of the Madonna stand in an impossibly tiny space: her cloak lifts in a way that suggests that there is no gravity, yet at first sight all does appear quite normal.

From the end of the sixteenth century Florence's importance as a centre of painting gradually diminished. Though the great Florentine tradition was certainly not yet extinguished —the seventeenth century was to witness the emergence of several great Florentine painters among whom Carlo Dolci is probably the finest—Florence came increasingly to resemble a provincial backwater and painters of talent began to seek their fortunes elsewhere. We will be relieved to see that this long and painful decline is not illustrated too obviously in the Uffizi. The remaining rooms devote little space to the tail end of the Florentine school and contain instead a dazzling collection of pictures by painters from all over Europe. In Rooms 34 and 35 we find Veronese, Tintoretto and the late sixteenth century in Venice and further down the corridor great paintings by northern European artists such as Rubens, Van Dyck, Rembrandt or Ruysdael and, in the very last rooms, some paintings by eighteenth-century English artists.

But as interesting as these paintings undoubtedly are, by this stage our capacity to comprehend anything more demanding than a cappuccino in the Piazza della Signoria is probably minimal and my advice is now to walk through the next four rooms without so much as glancing at a painting, turn left in the corridor and follow the signs for the exit. So ends a rapid visit to one of the great galleries of the world.

Map 5
The Medici, S. Lorenzo
and S. Marco

1. Palazzo Medici-Riccardi
2. S. Lorenzo
3. Medici Chapels
4. Cenacolo di Fuligno
5. Mercato Centrale
6. S. Apollonia
7. S. Marco
8. Chiostro dello Scalzo
9. Palazzo Pandolfini

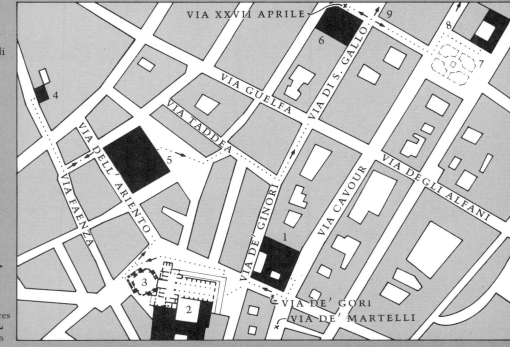

VIA XXVII APRILE

VIA GUELFA

VIA DI S. GALLO

VIA TADDEA

VIA DELL' ARIENTO

VIA FAENZA

VIA DE' GINORI

VIA CAVOUR

VIA DEGLI ALFANI

VIA DE' GORI

VIA DE' MARTELLI

N

0   50   100 150 metres

200 yards

5

THE MEDICI, S. LORENZO
—and—
S. MARCO

✤ If we walk a few hundred yards north up Via de' Martelli from the Duomo and enter Via Cavour we shall arrive at the doors of a large, imposing palazzo that looks at first sight very much like many other large and imposing palazzi all over Florence, but is of much greater interest than them all. For this is **Palazzo Medici-Riccardi** built and lived in by the first important members of that remarkable family who for better or worse dominated Florence, with only two short breaks, for three hundred years and whose history in that time is the history of the state itself. Though a legend long before they became extinct, their origins are shrouded in mystery. When Grand Dukes, the Medici fabricated their early history to suggest that they arrived in Florence as knights in Charlemagne's army, but the reality is certainly more prosaic. The Medici seem to have been small landowners and (even more painful for their Grand Ducal descendants for whom genealogy had an extraordinary importance) pharmacists living in the country north of Fiesole before they arrived in Florence sometime in the thirteenth century and settled near S. Lorenzo. By the sixteenth century they had risen to become princes of the Empire linked by marriage to the most important royal houses of Europe, producing a pair of Popes and two Queens of France, and amassing one of the world's greatest collections of art. Few families can claim a more spectacular history.

Many things—luck, money and skill among them—contributed to their dazzling rise but it would all have been impossible without the political acumen of the man who built this Palazzo and founded the political fortunes of the Medici, Cosimo 'il Vecchio' (1389–1464). He became the effective ruler of Florence from October 1434 when he returned from exile to be elected chief citizen of the Republic. At his death in 1464 he was unofficially succeeded by his more pedestrian and chronically arthritic son Piero 'the Gouty' who fortunately survived him by only three years, thus making way for the most fascinating Medici of them all—Lorenzo (1449–1492), usually called 'the Magnificent'. Though Lorenzo's magnificence is something of a contentious issue—many have seen him simply as a rather more ruthless if less efficient mafia leader than his father and grandfather—between them they presided over what can with some justification be called the Florentine golden age.

The façade of the Palazzo Medici-Riccardi (designed by Michelozzo and built between 1445 and 1455) is now twice its original length owing to some grand additions made at the end of the seventeenth century, and in order to imagine it as it once looked you must mentally block out the right half. When completed, the palazzo was by far the largest private residence in Florence. By the standards of the time it cost a staggeringly large sum, and twenty different houses were demolished to create its site. Bearing all this in mind, a story related by Vasari about Cosimo's instructions to his architect to build something 'modest and unpretentious' can be taken with a large pinch of salt.

Unfortunately it was the façade of the Palazzo Medici and not that of the roughly contemporary and much more interesting Palazzo Rucellai that became the model for Florentine domestic architecture over the next 150 years. For some reason it was not pilasters and architraves that fired the imagination of Florentine builders but massive rusticated blocks giving what Ruskin described as a thoroughly 'Newgate-like' effect. This is generally explained as 'proof of the overriding need for defence in fifteenth-century Tuscany', though it is difficult to see that the rustication on the façades, which becomes progressively smoother on each storey, does anything but facilitate climbing the walls for any potential attacker!

During the life of Lorenzo the Magnificent the interior of the palazzo must have seemed a garden of delights. Donatello's *Judith* majestically hacked off the head of *Holofernes* in the courtyard; his *David* stood in the garden surrounded by bushes cut to resemble the animals that the Medici liked to hunt on their estates in the Mugello. On the piano nobile the rooms were hung with Uccellos and Fra Angelicos. Today, except to those with the most enviable powers of imagination, this world seems a little distant. Stepping into the courtyard we see not the work of Donatello but the rugged Carabinieri guarding the city Prefect who now uses the palazzo as his office. There is only one room that remains as it was in the fifteenth century—the chapel with its ravishing frescoes of the *Journey of the Magi* by Benozzo Gozzoli (opening times, see p. 230). To reach it you take the staircase to the right of the entrance.

Entering the chapel is not entirely unlike being able to step inside one of the pages from the Duc de Berry's book of *Trés Riches Heures*. Though painted in 1459, Gozzoli's frescoes show little influence from the work of Masaccio or Donatello and are more reminiscent of the decorative if by then faintly old-fashioned International Gothic style. The three walls facing the altar are entirely covered by an ideal spring landscape and, across each of them, one of the Three Kings leads a procession to Bethlehem, following the Star up on the ceiling. The country in which it is set is made up, says Ruskin '... of roses and pomegranates, each drawn to the last rib and vein [which] twine themselves in perfect order about delicate trellisses; broad stones, pines and cypresses overshadow them.' He found the sky no less enchanting: '... bright birds hover here and there ... and groups of angels, hand joined with hand and wing with wing glide and float through the glades of the entangled forest.' What usually catches the eye is not the landscape but the exotic figures and animals in the procession—the giraffe, a camel, greyhounds, horses and, of course, the three magnificent kings arrayed in cloth of gold and oriental head-dresses.

Though not the most important artist of the mid-quattrocento (most of the figures in the procession are lifted from *The Adoration of the Magi* by Gentile da Fabriano now in the Uffizi), Gozzoli is certainly the most enchanting.

These paintings are surrounded by an undergrowth of myth no less charming and romantic than the paintings themselves: that the kings are really the Byzantine Emperors who visited Florence in 1440 for a disastrous council which failed to unite the Eastern and Western Churches, that the procession is their baggage train as it sets off for Constantinople from Florence and that the angelic looking young prince on the right wall is none other than Lorenzo the Magnificent (who was ten years old when it was painted). Sadly they all seem to be untrue. Could the Medici really have wished to be permanently reminded of such a disastrous council? And could Lorenzo, in every known portrait an unattractive man with a large nose and protruding cleft chin, ever have looked so angelic as a child?

There is one other room in the Palazzo Medici-Riccardi that is open to the public and transports us to a very different era. The painted Galleria (to reach which we take the smaller staircase on the right side of the courtyard) by the Neapolitan artist Luca Giordano (1632–1705) was painted in 1683. By then the palazzo had been bought and extended by the Riccardi, an immensely rich family who took themselves only a little less seriously than the Medici—who by now were Grand Dukes and living in Palazzo Pitti.

The Riccardi ran their palazzo as an alternative court throughout the eighteenth century, all the while collecting paintings, books and furniture. Theirs is probably the most inspired domestic baroque interior in Florence. Light pours in through the windows on the left and is sent shimmering in all directions by huge sheets of painted mirror to the right. The ceiling, supported by a regiment of athletic cherubs, swirls up into the clouds where, inevitably, we find the Medici apotheosised among coronets and Medicean heraldic *palle*. As by this stage they were in full decline and looking very unlike the divine creatures up here in the clouds, the subject is more than faintly absurd.

But the Riccardi reign of splendour came to an ignominious end in 1809 when, ruined by the financial demands of Napoleon, their possessions were auctioned in the Mercato Nuovo in a sale that lasted three days.

* * *

From the windows of the gallery we can see the top of the Medici church of S. Lorenzo, where, with the exception of the Popes and the two French Queens, every distinguished member of the family is buried. To reach the church turn right out of the entrance to Palazzo Medici-Riccardi, turn right again into Via de' Gori, walk on another fifty yards and you find yourself in Piazza S. Lorenzo (20) beside Bandinelli's painfully unattractive statue of Giovanni delle Bande Nere, who died a heroic death fighting Charles V—the Emperor, paradoxically, who was to make his son Duke of Tuscany. In the first quarter of the sixteenth century a succession of important architects were asked to draw up designs for a façade to the church, including Michelangelo, but as we can see, none of them was even begun. Throughout that time Medicean interests in Florence were

20

kept alive by the two Medici Popes and, as rich as Leo X and Clement VII were, they could never spare the sums of money required to build a façade on this scale.

S. Lorenzo was designed by Filippo Brunelleschi and begun in 1419, though it was completed long after his death. It is the first of his two great basilicas, the second being S. Spirito. Its plan is conventional and like that of S. Croce and S. Maria Novella is based on the Latin cross, though the transepts are unusually shallow and chapels recede from the side aisles. From a point of view of architectural history the most important part of the church, where Brunelleschi's genius can most profitably be observed, is a smallish room off the left transept called the Old Sacristy.

It was built in 1421–8, before the rest of the church had been begun, and was paid for entirely by the Medici as a burial chapel for Giovanni de' Bicci de' Medici, Cosimo il Vecchio's father and the founder of the Medicean financial empire. Conceived around ideas of arithmetical proportion, it is sometimes called 'the first building of the Renaissance' though there is a slightly earlier and suspiciously familiar baptistery in Padua that Brunelleschi had almost certainly seen before he began this in 1421. It is more subtle and sophisticated than it at first appears: the room is a perfect cube, the walls are divided into thirds, each being equal to the radius of the delicate hemispherical 'umbrella dome' of the ceiling. This is the first instance of a strikingly successful decorative scheme that Brunelleschi used throughout his career and that was to be copied by Florentine architects until this century. The walls are painted white, but fine, taut lines of grey pietra serena outline the principal architectural members. There are many signs, however, that Brunelleschi was not yet the master of his own innovations. There is, for instance, something strangely uncomfortable about the pilasters and cornice when they arrive at a corner. Most of these problems were only to be solved by the next generation of architects.

As with most of Brunelleschi's buildings, later generations have not treated the Old Sacristy with much respect. Andrea del Verrocchio found the original entrance the perfect position for his monument to Piero the Gouty and his brother

Giovanni (1472; the red porphyry coffin on gilded lion's-paw feet is one of the finest pieces of craftsmanship in Florence of its date). With astounding insensitivity he closed the entrance but for structural reasons was obliged to squeeze the new door uncomfortably into one corner, rather spoiling the fragile and calculated elegance of the room.

S. Lorenzo is a treasure house of important works of art and we are now faced with a serious *embarras de choix*. There is a particularly fine early Mannerist painting, *The Marriage of the Virgin* (1523) in the second chapel to the right, by Rosso Fiorentino. In the chapel to the right of the Old Sacristy hangs a good painting of *St Anthony Abbot, St Leonard and St Julian* attributed to the School of Ghirlandaio. Directly opposite this chapel is a late nineteenth-century Monument to Donatello beneath which the artist is buried and above which is a fine Filippo Lippi. But the finest and most moving works here are the bronze pulpits in the nave, the very last works of Donatello. Like some other artists of the highest calibre— Michelangelo, for instance, or Titian—Donatello lived, by the standards of Renaissance Italy, to be a

very old man indeed. Like them he continued to work right up until he died—in his case at the age of 80—and in those last years produced masterpieces radically different from anything else in his entire *oeuvre*. These panels, made in about 1460, have a wild, free, confused violence about them. His modelling becomes more free and more expressive than in any earlier work and in places portrays scenes of savage, almost insane, violence. Rather as Titian applied the paint to his last pictures with his fingers in impressionistic smears, turning his back on a lifetime of scrupulously professional technique, here Donatello ignores every convention and rule of fifteenth-century sculpture. In the *Lamentation* (left pulpit, facing aisle) two bodies are cut in half by the frame and the mourners stand about in overcrowded, wailing groups. In the scene beside it the perspective moves in and out at random. If you look carefully at the surface of the bronze, it has been savagely cut with a chisel after modelling and it is not hard to imagine the infirm, pathetic old man desperately trying to complete every panel before he died, inspired by a fierce new lease of creative imagination.

*or Renoir with his penis!

On the first floor of the S. Lorenzo cloisters (reached by taking the door from the southern side of the nave immediately to your right) is the **Laurentian library** (opening times, see p. 231). It was designed by Michelangelo and is high Renaissance architecture at its grandest and most flamboyant. Most of the vestibule is taken up by the fabulous staircase that gives the impression of rushing, or flowing down from the library to which it leads. By climbing the stairs you can experience the intended contrast between the soaring verticals of the staircase vestibule and the highly disciplined, ordered horizontals of the library which is conceived as a sequence of cubes in which the structure is linked to the decoration in a more effective way than had yet been achieved by any other Renaissance architect. The decoration of the walls is echoed both on the ceiling and in the mosaic floor of the central aisle, thus drawing the eye along the length of the room.

Commissioned by Clement VII, the library still contains the magnificent collection of books and manuscripts assembled by Cosimo il Vecchio and Lorenzo the Magnificent. The extravagance of the building speaks for the pride which the Medici took in their library, probably the finest of its kind outside the Vatican, which they formed by expending large sums of money and equivalent amounts of energy. Cosimo il Vecchio was sensible enough to make free loans to a certain Niccolò Niccoli, a charmingly unworldly collector and the only fifteenth-century Florentine of whom I have ever heard with no interest whatsoever in making money. Ignoring his family business, he spent his considerable inheritance on books and manuscripts that he unearthed from monastic libraries all over Germany, France and Italy. At his death Cosimo naturally seized the most valuable part of his collection and installed it in the Palazzo Medici-Riccardi. Cosimo also employed a particularly unscrupulous and effective agent called Niccolò Poggio who, by using generous bribes, managed to discover and obtain a copy of Pliny's *Natural History* from a monastery in Lübeck, Cicero's *Orations* in France and Tacitus' *Histories* somewhere else. They miraculously survived the ransack of the palazzo in 1494 and were then moved to S. Marco where they managed to survive another ransacking mob, this time ousting not the Medici but Savonarola, before being taken to Rome in 1508. That is probably where they would have stayed had Clement VII not decided to return them to Florence in the 1520s and built this library to house them. Until the 1930s the books were still kept on the desks, fastened by little chains and protected from the light by large velvet covers. Though they are now kept in a room out of sight, you can still ask to be shown some illuminated manuscripts—though some of the library's more bizarre treasures, like the finger of Galileo preserved in a jar that was shown to Lady Blessington in 1817, seem to have disappeared.

The entrance to the most famous of the sights in S. Lorenzo, the **Medici tombs**, at the other end of the building and reached by walking round the outside of the church (opening times, see p. 231, ask for tickets to the New Sacristy crypt at the ticket desk) is appropriately funereal. We walk through the low dark crypt, up some steps, then into an underlit corridor before reaching what is, with the possible exception of the Sistine chapel ceiling, Michelangelo's most awe-inspiringly wonderful creation, the New Sacristy.

One of the most profoundly depressing and yet fascinating creations of the high Renaissance in Italy, the New Sacristy was begun in 1521, almost a century later than Brunelleschi's Old Sacristy, to which it bears many similarities—being decorated in the same materials and of the same size only taller. But whereas one is an early and cautious experiment with the principles of classical architecture, this is a fully mature exercise that for the first time rejects many of the rules that govern the use of the classical 'orders'. Michelangelo takes liberties with the classical vocabulary that Brunelleschi would have thought horrendous—he places heavy tabernacles above voids, gives the architectural elements no structural function, tapers windows, and treats the walls, in fact, like a vast piece of sculpture.

The first impression that strikes the visitor to this strange palace of the dead is of its intense stillness—perhaps better described as its ghostly calm. In part this is due to ingenious tricks with the light, which falls like an even grey cloud from high windows giving everything a touch of the ethereal. The tombs are on the right and left walls. Above them, perched in niches and dressed in the uniforms of patrician Roman generals, are the two Medici, Giuliano, Duke of Nemours (right), and Lorenzo, Duke of Urbino (left) who stare down at Michelangelo's *Madonna and Child* (1521).

Ironically the greatest of Renaissance tomb chambers is all, nominally at least, to the glory of two thoroughly inglorious people, perhaps the least impressive pair of the entire dynasty. Both were the creations of Pope Leo X. Giuliano ruled Florence in an ineffectual sort of way for a year in 1512. His nephew Lorenzo, to the right, is more interesting only because he is the father of Catherine de' Medici, whom Clement VII managed to marry off to the King of France. But just as the real purpose of the tombs was not to honour the memory of the two dead men themselves but to proclaim the importance of their family, so these statues are not intended as portraits but represent idealised states of the mind. Giuliano symbolises the Active Life, Lorenzo, with his head in his hand, the Contemplative Life.

A development of the same idea, the four statues sprawled beneath them represent times of day. Beneath Lorenzo are *Dawn* (the female figure to his right) who seems to be only half awake and lethargic, and *Dusk* who appears drowsy and on the point of sleep. *Day* and *Night* beneath Giuliano are considered some of Michelangelo's most expressive and successful sculptures. *Night* is the exhausted, tortured woman whose breasts hang limp from her chest and whose stomach is creased with the lines of age. She contrasts with *Day* whose body is girded with steel muscles, and who glares in defiance across Herculean shoulders. One thing, at least, is obvious—that they are intended to portray the passage of time and even the misery of existence. All wear expressions of intense, fathomless grief.

In the crypt are recently discovered drawings by Michelangelo thought to have been executed as he lay in hiding during 1527.

The Cappella dei Principi, begun in 1602 to the designs of Don Giovanni de' Medici, a talented illegitimate son of Cosimo I, is perhaps less difficult to understand. A product of the Medici at their most comically yet admirably fantastic and insane, it was begun in the early seventeenth century and planned on a heroic scale of princely magnificence. As extraordinarily ostentatious as it now seems, it is only partially complete. Had it been finished as first envisaged, the Grand Dukes would have been sculpted in nothing so pedestrian as gilded bronze but from translucent, coloured semi-precious stone; the internal façades, covering rather more than an acre, were to be entirely encrusted with inlaid *pietre dure* and the ceiling would have been an ecstatic baroque fantasy representing the Medici in apotheosis. Only the lower level of the walls, with their inlaid heraldic arms of the sixteen Tuscan cities, are completed as intended.

The construction and decoration of their mausoleum was a source of enormous pleasure and pride to the Medici, but it has seldom been greatly admired by others. Byron thought it 'fine frippery in slabs of various expensive stones to commemorate 50 rotten and forgotten carcasses'. It was, however, one of the few things that caught the attention of Oscar Wilde when he came to Florence in the 1870s. Teams of craftsmen worked here for more than a century, covering the walls with inlaid *pietre dure*. Completing it before her death became the obsession of Anna Maria, the last of the Medici; but at her death in 1743 it was still unfinished, and despite intermittent work in the eighteenth and the nineteenth centuries it remains so.

All the Medici Grand Dukes and three of the Habsburg/Lorraine Grand Dukes are buried in the Cappella dei Principi. Cosimo I's tomb faces the entrance. The large gilded bronze figures of ~~Francesco I~~ and Cosimo II above the tombs to his right are by Pietro Tacca, Giambologna's most talented pupil. However, all of their coffins are in the vault below. The Grand Dukes were buried with all the magnificence that one might expect. Like pharaohs they were interred carrying all the essentials for the world to come—holding sceptres, wearing gold crowns and wrapped in their finest state robes. The inevitable result is that the tombs, like the pyramids, have been repeatedly robbed, most effectively by Napoleon's *Armée d'Italie* in 1802.

✱ Ferdinand I

In order to find out just what still remained inside their coffins they were officially opened after a prayer of blessing in the presence of Pope Pius IX who made a special trip up from Rome in 1857. Watched by soldiers of what was still the Grand Ducal guard, a committee of clerical and civil servants found that only two tombs had remained unviolated, those of the last two Grand Dukes, Cosimo III and Gian Gastone. Their report makes a grim but strangely fascinating read. Eleonora, of Toledo, wife of Cosimo I, was buried in the same dress that she wears in her portrait by Bronzino in The Tribuna. Giovanni delle Bande Nere was found in his famous black armour. The doctors, shown his amputated leg, were not much surprised that he had died from the operation.

*   *   *

For a complete change of atmosphere we now pay a visit to the Mercato Centrale, to reach which we only have to turn right from the exit of the Medici chapels and walk a short way up the first street on the left, the busy Via dell' Ariento, which is full of stalls and known to Florentines as 'Shanghai'. The diligent sightseer, however, will first visit the Cenacolo di Fuligno, a charming refectory on the street running parallel and to the west of Via dell' Ariento, at Via Faenza 42 (about three hundred yards up that street on the right) with a fine *Last Supper* by Perugino, one of the least visited great paintings in Florence.

Built in the 1870s, the iron and glass Mercato (21) is, since the tragic destruction of Les Halles in Paris, the finest surviving building of its kind in Europe. It was built as a bright and clean new shopping centre to replace the Mercato Vecchio, now the Piazza della Repubblica. For the first ten years of its life it was an embarrassing white elephant as the Mercato Vecchio stall holders refused to leave their familiar and more picturesque squalor. They were eventually persuaded to make the transition when the demolition squads arrived. It remains as it must have been then—a curious mixture of the beautiful and the sordid. Beside exquisite scented flowers there are great sides of dripping red pig and calf; next to mountains of oranges, purple asparagus, huge black *funghi porcini* and bunches of basil or jacaranda there are severed heads of wild boar (particularly valued for their brains) and strings of tiny, brightly coloured birds trapped in the contado and just waiting to be turned into a casserole. There are cafés at the other side of the market where the world of tourist Florence seems very far distant. Contadini, who probably arrived here before dawn in their noisy little three-wheeled vespas, sit at tables drinking *amari* and *espressi*.

From the north-east corner of the Mercato Centrale take Via Rosina, turn right again into Via Taddea and you arrive in Via de' Ginori which contains the larger part of Florence's university and some good sixteenth-century palazzi (at No. 15, Palazzo Taddei, where the Michelangelo tondo now in the Royal Academy used to hang over the door, at No. 11, Palazzo Ginori and at No. 9, Palazzo Montauto). Here turn left and walk to Via XXVII Aprile where, if you turn left again, you will arrive at the **convent of Sant' Apollonia** (the first door on the left, at No. 1. Ring bell for admission). The *Last Supper* (1444) in the Refectory is the masterpiece of Andrea del Castagno, a highly innovative artist who played an important role in the spread of early Renaissance ideas to the north

of Italy and to Venice. Here you see the origin of ideas that were later to be developed by Ghirlandaio and then by Leonardo da Vinci. The scene is set in a marbled pictorial space which appears to extend from the real space of the refectory.

*   *   *

Via XXVII Aprile runs east into Piazza S. Marco. Though the Piazza is less of a feast to the eye than its Venetian namesake, on its north side stands one of the really great and moving small museums in Florence and indeed in the world—the Dominican **friary of S. Marco** (opening times, see p. 231) containing the most important frescoes and panel paintings by Fra Angelico (1387–1455). A first visit is one of the great experiences of a lifetime. The building remains unaltered from the fifteenth century and harmonises in an almost magical way with the paintings that it contains, providing the visitor with an extraordinary impression that he is entering the world of the artist and the life of the monastic order in which he lived.

Before looking at any of his paintings we should pause for a minute in the Piazza or sit down in the cloister and read for a minute about the history of both the painter and the building. For the existence of S. Marco we have to thank the Medici. Its foundation was the most fortunate and perhaps the most generous philanthropic gesture of Cosimo il Vecchio, who began to enlarge the friary soon after his return from exile in 1434 using Michelozzo, his favourite architect. The simple, elegant austerity of his design reflects the life of the order for which it was intended—a particularly strict reformed sect of the Dominicans called the Observants whose founder had urged Christians not only to reject unnecessary material comforts but to ignore the literature of antiquity and read only the 'Holy writ, in which the Lord has laid out the true poetry of wisdom and the true eloquence of the spirit of truth'.

This, it must be admitted, is not usually the sort of thing that great painters thrive on, but Fra Angelico is an exception. Unlike his contemporary Fra Filippo Lippi, to whom he might be described as a polar opposite, he was no Bohemian; an ascetic monastic life seems to have been very much to his taste. Even if we do not believe every word of Vasari's character sketch of which I quote this passage '. . . some say that Fra Giovanni [Angelico] never took up a brush without the tears coursing down his cheeks, while the goodness of his sincere and great soul in religion may be seen from the attitudes of his figures . . .' there is no reason to doubt that he was of a devout, saintly character. As Vasari says, the most striking quality of his painting is its deeply felt spirituality. It is this that first strikes the visitor who enters the Ospizio dei Pellegrini, the room on the entrance-side of the courtyard, containing some of his greatest work.

Looking at these paintings, it is equally obvious that Fra Angelico cannot be dismissed merely as a painter of late 'primitives' for he was a highly sophisticated artist who despite initial appearances absorbed much from the techniques of his contemporaries and in particular from the work of Masaccio at the Brancacci Chapel in the Carmine. Two great altarpieces of the *Deposition* (painted for S. Trinita in 1435) at the near end, and the *Last Judgment* (c.1430) flooded with light, burnished with brilliant colour and painted with a meticulous attention to detail, reveal the monumental, sculptural aspects of his art. The compositions are simply conceived but their effect of harmony and unity is dependent on a subtle use of the newly discovered techniques of artificial perspective.

In the 35 *Scenes from the Life of Christ* you see a side of Fra Angelico often forgotten—his skill as a painter of landscapes. His grey-brown hills receding into space, horizontal wispy bands of cloud and flaking wall surfaces formed Proust's image of Tuscany, a land that he never visited but described lovingly in *Swann's Way*.

At the far side of the courtyard, in the Sala Capitolare, is Fra Angelico's *Crucifixion* (1442), which has been effectively destroyed by deterioration and restoration. All the blue background has been removed, and the figures of the saints completely repainted. It is not one of his most successful paintings, designed not so much to please the eye as to expound the Observants' intellectual concept of the Church. 'It remains a manifesto that falls short of a work of art,' writes Sir John Pope-Hennessy, so we shall move on to the refectory where there is a *Last Supper* by Domenico

Ghirlandaio, before climbing the stairs to the first floor to see Fra Angelico's more expressive and emotive frescoes painted between 1442 and 1447 when he was called to Rome by the Papacy to decorate St Peter's in his final years.

At the top of the stairs is perhaps the most famous of all Fra Angelico's paintings, the *Annunciation*, finished before he began the enormous task of painting, with assistants, the 44 different friar's cells around the courtyard. His own hand can be seen in about a quarter of that number and most of these are on the eastern side of the cloister (to the left at the top of the staircase) in cells 1–9.

In these cells the friars would spend the larger part of their lives, and the paintings in them are intended not as decoration but as aids to contemplation, and were intended to constantly remind the occupant of the cell of the scene, or rather the mystery, that they describe. They are one of those works of art that can only be fully appreciated in the original. For as soon as one enters a cell one immediately grasps their real purpose. In each case the scene is represented on the window wall opposite the door, and the wall thus contains two apertures, one opening on to the physical and the other into the spiritual world. They are the only item of colour in an otherwise small, white room and their impact is enormous. It is an experience that you can repeat in all the cells, though the painting in those facing the courtyard is clearly of a lower standard.

Fra Angelico supervised a team of assistants on these paintings, but is thought to have completed the following with little or no assistance: *Noli me Tangere* in cell 1; the *Annunciation* in cell 3, which is simpler but seems more deeply felt than the one at the top of the stairs. Notice the change of setting—instead of a Brunelleschian loggia he paints a bare room enclosed by a windowless wall, which emphasises the enclosure of the cell itself; the *Transfiguration* in cell 6; the *Crowning with Thorns* in cell 7 and the *Coronation of the Virgin* in cell 9.

There are two particularly large and interesting cells, and these are at opposite ends of the corridor. One was the cell of the prior, and we reach it by walking to the end of the southern side of the cloister. Its most famous and frightening occupant was Girolamo Savonarola (1452–1498) who became prior in 1491 at the request of Lorenzo the Magnificent, though his indictments of materialism and his exhortations on the importance of constitutional government contributed to the exile of the Medici three years later. One of many fifteenth-century puritanical religious reformers, he made his reputation as a powerful orator, first in the church of S. Marco and then in the Duomo. After the expulsion of the Medici he became a prominent supporter of a government that demanded rigorous religious orthodoxy and denounced the evils of Medicean Florence. His reign ended in 1498 after four years, when a mob besieged the convent and dragged Savonarola off to be imprisoned, tortured, tried and then later executed on the Piazza della Signoria.

Retracing our steps to the top of the staircase and then continuing along the corridor, we pass on the left the S. Marco library where, says Lord Clark, 'humanists made discoveries that would alter the course of history with an explosion not of matter but of mind'. Some may feel that this is a romanticised view of the importance of the classical rediscovery in the Renaissance but few will fail to find it one of the most elegant and beautiful pieces of fifteenth-century Florentine architecture. Its books are now mainly in the Laurentian Library. At the far end of this corridor on the right is the cell that was occasionally used by S. Marco's patron, Cosimo il Vecchio. Rather larger than the other cells, it was reserved for his own use and as a room for important visitors. On the wall facing the door is an *Adoration of the Magi* thought to be mainly by the hand of Fra Angelico, but heavily repainted in the nineteenth century.

From the window in Cosimo's cell you look east across the northern part of Florence, a quarter that conceals many delights. At 69 Via Cavour is the **Chiostro dello Scalzo**, a cloister painted (between 1511 and 1526) in grisaille by Andrea del Sarto and Franciabigio with scenes reflecting the *Four Cardinal Virtues* and the *Life of the Baptist*. These make an interesting contrast to the polychrome frescoes by the same artist in SS. Annunziata (see page 199). At the end of Via S. Gallo (No. 74) stands the **Palazzo Pandolfini**, a beautiful early sixteenth-century palazzo built for a bishop and a friend of the Medici Popes. It is the only work of architecture by Raphael in Florence.

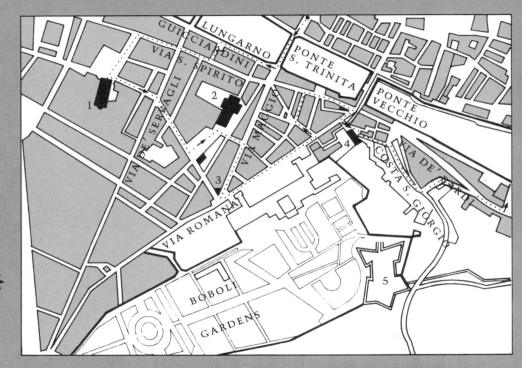

Map 6
The Oltrarno (West)

1. S. Maria del Carmine
2. S. Spirito
3. Casa Guidi
4. S. Felicità
5. Forte del Belvedere

N

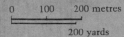

0   100   200 metres

200 yards

6

THE OLTRARNO

✤ For roughly a century, from the decade of the Brownings to the twilight years of Berenson, Florence was one of the social capitals of Europe. For Russians and Americans, French, Germans and particularly for the English it became the quintessence of everything pleasurably Italian. Its pace was unhurried, its prices gloriously cheap, its streets safe and its social season rivalled only in London, Paris, Petersburg and Vienna. Pleasantly cut off from the European mainstream yet less provincial than Naples or Rome, it became the home of an expatriate community that by 1914 was estimated at between 35,000 and 40,000 people at the height of the season and of a way of life that can still be pleasurably savoured in novels such as Anatole France's *Le Lys Rouge* or Ronald Firbank's highly amusing but little-known play *The Princess Zubaroff.*

Though that world has long since disappeared, there are places where a connection with the recent past seems particularly strong, and nowhere more so than where the most fashionable and expensive street in Florence, Via Tornabuoni, turns into Piazza S. Trinita. (22) Every aesthete worthy of the name, from the Frères Goncourt and Oscar Wilde to Harold Acton and the Sitwells, seems to have had long, lazy lunches or amusing gossipy teas at Doney's, between us and the golden

22

hulk of the Palazzo Strozzi. Just around the corner in the Lungarno Corsini used to be Orioli's bookshop, where D. H. Lawrence published the first edition of *Lady Chatterley's Lover* in 1927. The top floor of the late medieval Palazzo Buondelmonte (to the far right of the photograph on this page) was once the most famous reading room in Italy and the centre of intellectual life in Florence during most of the nineteenth century. It was used by Leopardi, that most lyrically pessimistic of all Italian poets, and by Robert Browning, though not by his wife Elizabeth as, to her disgust, the efficient but male-chauvinistic Genevan founder of the library called Gian Pietro Vieusseux did not permit female members.

The architecturally more inspiring Palazzo Bartolini-Salimbeni to its left, between Via delle Terme and Via Porta Rossa (now the French Consulate, designed by Baccio d'Agnolo and built in 1520–30), is the first and one of the last Florentine palazzi with high Renaissance or 'Roman' pretensions. Until the 1930s it was the smartest hotel in the city, despite the ominous inscription '*Per non dormire*' on the upstairs windows.

Piazza S. Trinita is an odd jumble of buildings, but it is lent a certain dignity and elegance by the antique marble column in its centre which comes from the Baths of Caracalla in Rome. It was floated and dragged here with immense labour in 1554 and supposedly marks the spot where Cosimo I, aged twenty, heard the good news of a victory over his opponents that was to establish the Medici as absolute rulers of Tuscany for the next two hundred years. From the point of view of urban planning he could hardly have chosen a better place to stand, as it links up two impressive vistas—one to the north up Via Tornabuoni to Piazza Antinori, the other south over the Ponte S. Trinita and down Via Maggio. It makes an excellent place to begin a walk through that most lively and colourful part of Florence—the Oltrarno.

Leaving Palazzo Ferroni (bought in 1938 for only three million lire by Salvatore Ferragamo, the outstanding Italian shoe designer of this century and still the headquarters of his company), on the left and the church of S. Trinita (see page 190) on the right, we arrive at the Arno. Though the panorama of palaces and bridges, domes, spires and more bridges stretching into the distance in both directions with green hills high in the background, rarely disappoints the visitor, the river itself often does. Primed with highly coloured descriptions like that in Elizabeth Barrett Browning's *Casa Guidi Windows*:

'. . . I can but muse upon this shore
Of golden Arno as it shoots away
Through Florence' heart beneath her bridges
 four:
Bent bridges, seeming to strain like bows,
And tremble with the arrowy undertide
Shoots on and cleaves the marble as it goes . . .'

they arrive expecting it to look something like the Nile in its upper reaches and usually find, if it is any time between May and October, a desiccated river-bed covered in a patchwork of weeds. In spring and autumn, however, it can look impressive and about thrice in every two centuries it floods with extraordinary violence. The intervening periods between these floods are just long enough to make the Florentines feel that they will never happen again and thus they are always caught unprepared. That was certainly true on the last occasion—on 18th November 1966—when both the Uffizi and the Biblioteca Nazionale suffered since they used their ground floors and basements for storage.

If the two statues on the end of the Ponte S. Trinita's parapet look rather battered it is because they were blown up, like the bridge, in August 1944. After the war they were pieced together, though the head of the *Primavera* (by a French pupil of Giambologna called Pietro Francavilla, 1583) on the left was only discovered in 1962 and the right arm in 1980. Despite horrendous central government plans for a reinforced concrete bridge 'in the spirit' of the one destroyed, the superb reconstruction we see was achieved with the help of an international subscription, the original plans, sixteenth-century tools and new stone from a quarry reopened in the Boboli. Unfortunately the same efforts were not made to rebuild accurately the medieval *borghi* at either end of the Ponte Vecchio, which look very much 'in the spirit' of the early 1950s.

Though less famous than the Ponte Vecchio, its older neighbour, the **Ponte S. Trinita** is a much more subtle and sophisticated bridge and the best possible combination of art with engineering. Its three arches leap across the river with astounding grace and, though they seem perilously thin at their top edge, have withstood countless devastating floods, the weight of Napoleon's artillery and of a great many overladen Florentine buses.

The attribution of its design is one of those never-ending art-historical controversies to which there will probably never be any real solution. Though all the conventional sources credit it to Ammanati, a sculptor/architect almost as prolific as his contemporary Giorgio Vasari, it seems so out of character with the rest of his work, and so unusual in its inspiration, that the obvious temptation is to attribute the design to Michelangelo. But the only evidence for such an attractive theory is that the catenary or semi-elliptical arches on the bridge are identical to those on his Medici tombs in the New Sacristy at S. Lorenzo.

At the far side of the bridge we arrive in a busy little piazza that is the junction of no less than five different roads. Its most interesting building, immediately to the left, is the Palazzo Frescobaldi. It has a late seventeenth-century façade on what was a thirteenth-century palazzo that probably once looked rather similar to the Palazzo Ferroni on the other side of the river, and like it was intended as a fortress to guard the bridge. Above the entrance are portrait busts of four Medici Grand Dukes, and it was the second from the left, Francesco I, who commissioned the charming fountain by Buontalenti on the next street corner. In front of us is Via Maggio which is the largest and possibly (though the competition is intense) the noisiest street in the Oltrarno.

Turning right down the Lungarno Guicciardini we pass (at No. 1) the entrance to the Pensione Bartolini where most people wrongly suppose that E. M. Forster based the first chapters of *A Room with a View*. The next house but one was, during the eighteenth century, a well-known inn where Grand Tourists generally broke their journey for a few days before speeding on to sample the delights of antiquity in Rome. Its only long-term residents were those whose tastes were considered too decadent to be tolerated anywhere but in Florence.

At this point, midway between the Ponte S. Trinita and the Ponte alla Carraia, look across to the other side of the river and enjoy a captivating view that remains unchanged from the eighteenth century when it was engraved by Giuseppe Zocchi. (**23**, overleaf)

To the far left, across the river, is Palazzo Ricasoli, owned but never lived in by Bettino Ricasoli, the 'iron baron' who was twice Prime Minister of Italy in the 1860s. Possibly designed by Michelozzo in the first half of the fifteenth century, it is now more than five hundred years old and just about as solid as his castle of Brolio (that remained virtually undamaged despite 127 direct hits by shells in 1944) and as indelibly Tuscan as Ricasoli himself. It could scarcely provide a greater contrast with its neighbour—the lighter and more festive Palazzo Corsini, built in the late seventeenth century. If one is sombre, discreet and conservative the other is ostentatious and extravagant in the very spirit of the Roman baroque. Statues dance above a façade that seems to be more glass than wall, and the wings step forward

23

to enclose a courtyard which, with a little help from Zocchi and the imagination, one can picture as the setting for some sumptuous baroque entertainment.

The Corsini were the richest, grandest and most interesting Florentine noble family of the seventeenth and eighteenth centuries. They claimed to be able to ride from Florence to Rome on their own property, produced a succession of scholarly Cardinals, a Saint and, for good measure, Pope Clement XII in 1730, who commissioned, among other things, the Trevi fountain and the façade of S. Giovanni dei Fiorentini in Rome. His nephew, Prince Lorenzo Corsini, amassed the greater part of the pictures in the Corsini collection which still hang in the palazzo's famous gallery (which can be visited by appointment, see Appendix p. 221).

A few houses further to the right, in the grey building that is now the British Consulate, lived the most obscure of British Queens—Louise, Countess of Albany. She married the Young Pretender, 'Bonnie Prince Charlie', in 1766 as an alternative to spending the rest of her life in a convent, though by then he was, to quote from the *Dictionary of National Biography*, 'neither young nor bonny but a drunken old sot'. Within three years she had left him for a more amusing life in this palazzo with Vittorio Alfieri, the most distinguished Italian dramatist of his generation. Though Horace Walpole thought she had not 'a rag of royalty about her' she created the brightest salon in Florence, entertained both Byron and Stendhal and throughout her life, even when in England, insisted on being treated as Queen Louise, wife of Charles III, the true claimant to the British throne.

One of the best ways to get a feeling of what life was like in eighteenth-century Florence is to read the letters of Sir Horace Mann, the English envoy to Tuscany between 1740 and 1786, to his rather more witty and colourful friend Sir Horace Walpole. Though not everyone's choice for bedtime reading, they are full of interesting social trivia and gossip and give a good picture of Florence in an age when love had clearly become, as in *Tristram Shandy* '. . . not a sentiment but a situation'. He gave weekly parties at his house the Casa Manetti which is just around the corner at

No. 23 Via S. Spirito (turn your back on the Arno, walk down Via dei Geppi and turn right, it is the large house on the opposite side of the road). His guests were the Florentine nobility who, to judge from his letters, seem to have thought of little but their *cicisbei* (the lover/companion who played a curious but ubiquitous role in the social life of the Italian nobility in the eighteenth century), or the next masked ball, and nothing at all of putting Sir Horace's best wine glasses into their pockets as they left his parties. He was, however, never more than a competent diplomat and twice caused a minor panic in London by sending false alarms warning of the imminent arrival of Bonnie Prince Charlie in Scotland.

Mann's house is just about equidistant from the two largest churches in the Oltrarno—S. Maria del Carmine and S. Spirito, both extremely important, interesting and well worth seeing, though for very different reasons.

*   *   *

S. Maria del Carmine (continue along Via S. Spirito into Borgo S. Frediano, then take the first left into the Piazza del Carmine, the church is on the south side) makes a poor first impression. Behind an unfinished façade there is a strangely lugubrious late eighteenth-century nave which looks like a less elaborate version of rather earlier churches in Rome, though the ceiling is an impressive piece of *trompe l'oeil*. This was built following a fire in 1771 that gutted the original Gothic church, destroying frescoes by Giotto but sparing the two chapels in the transepts and the Sacristy. The **Brancacci Chapel** in the right transept contains what are arguably the most important paintings in Florence, a fresco cycle relating *Scenes from Genesis and the Life of St Peter*. At least five of the remaining scenes are wholly or largely by Masaccio, a painter whose life remains shrouded in mystery despite his enormous significance in the history of Florentine and European painting. Born in 1401 in a small town between Florence and Arezzo, he was well established and receiving important commissions by his early twenties, but his career lasted no more than a few years, for he died in Rome aged 26 or 27. These frescoes were probably painted at several different times between 1425 and 1427.

Like all his work they demonstrate a quite astonishing originality. Unlike his contemporaries, Masaccio was interested less in making elegant compositions with graceful, sinewy surface lines than in imparting a convincing portrayal of Man and the landscape, the air, the light and the objects of the natural world that surround him.

'Dust-bitten and ruined though his Brancacci frescoes now are, I never see them without the strongest stimulation of my tactile consciousness, I feel that I could touch every figure, that it would yield a definite resistance to my touch and that I would have to expend thus much effort to displace it and that I could walk around it,' wrote Bernard Berenson, describing these frescoes in the 1890s. Now that their long overdue restoration is (hopefully) complete and layers of overpainting have been removed exposing once again the greens, reds and blues, the rapid brush strokes and the details of the original frescoes, Berenson's impressions are easier to share. In the *Expulsion from Paradise* (on the left of the entrance arch) Adam and Eve have all the chiselled solidity of Donatello's sculp-ture in Or San Michele, and they make an interesting comparison with the weightless, if perhaps more elegant, Adam and Eve in the *Temptation* (at the opposite side of the arch) by Masolino, a successful if rather more conventional painter with whom Masaccio worked very closely. Masaccio imparts his figures with life and emotion in many ways—with a bold use of light and shade, with broad, confident brush strokes and by expressing their anguish in their physical gestures. Eve's head, for instance, is tilted back and her mouth is wide open to give a convincing impression that she is screaming, while Adam holds his head in his hands as if to hide his shame. Within fifty years such techniques and ideas had become standard in Florentine painting, but in 1425 they were revolutionary.

The most celebrated of Masaccio's Brancacci frescoes is *The Tribute Money* in the middle of the upper register on the left wall. Set in sunny, mountainous countryside that seems convincingly filled with light and space, this scene is remarkable both for its technical accomplishment and for the view of the world that it imparts. Man not only dominates the landscape around him but for the first time in Christian painting is presented on equal terms to Christ who stands in the midst of his Apostles.

Also by Masaccio are *St Peter Enthroned* (to the right of the altar, upper register), *St Peter Distributing Alms* (left of the altar, lower register) and *St Peter Healing the Sick with his Shadow* (right of the altar, lower register). Masolino is responsible for the rest of the upper register. The lower register was completed by Filippino Lippi in the late fifteenth century.

The Corsini Chapel in the opposite transept was decorated about 250 years later to provide a suitably opulent resting place for the newly canonised S. Andrea Corsini, a particularly pious thirteenth-century Bishop of Fiesole. The combined cost of canonisation and the chapel is said to have been so great that even the immensely rich Prince Corsini felt relieved that there was only one saint in his family and urged his children to content themselves in future simply with being holy.

Decorated (between 1675 and 1683) by the most talented and sought-after artists then working in Italy—the deep marble reliefs of Sant' Andrea as a man of prayer, as a man of action and a man of peace are by Foggini and the ceiling is by Luca Giordano—it is a rare example of the Florentine baroque taking wings to achieve something comparable to the work of Bernini in Rome.

If we turn right out of S. Maria del Carmine, walk down Via S. Monaca and recross Via de' Serragli to Via S. Agostino we find ourselves, suddenly, in the heart of the Oltrarno. All the streets to the right and left are residential and around us there are cafés, laundries and barber's shops where there always seems to be someone sprawled back, as if on a dentist's chair, while being shaved. The atmosphere feels more southern Italian than anywhere else in Florence, and the Piazza S. Spirito, a little further on, has all the run-down, noisy, seedy, amiable charm of parts of Naples or Palermo. If it is before midday there will be a small market of half a dozen carts piled high with artichokes or purple figs and mushrooms depending on the season; if it is a warm summer evening there will probably be a group of old men sitting and smoking on the benches of the Palazzo Guadagni (on the corner with Via Mazzetta, No. 10), the finest example of domestic architecture on this side of the river (attrib. Baccio d'Agnolo 1501–9). The loggiaed top floor has long been a charming pensione that should have inspired at least a dozen novels but for some reason has not. It is on its loggia that most of this guide has been written. From the corner of the palazzo hangs a fine original iron lantern.

*   *   *

At this end of the piazza stands the inevitable nineteenth-century statue to a hero of the Risorgimento, in this case a worthy reformer called Cosimo Ridolfi who among many other momentous achievements was responsible for having gas light installed in the Florentine streets in the 1830s. At the far end of the piazza is the unfinished façade of Brunelleschi's last and greatest church, **S. Spirito**, which architects have been itching to embellish with something more elaborate ever since it was finished at the end of the fifteenth century. More than one competition has been held with the aim of producing a scheme of real quality, though fortunately no patron has ever come forward with adequate supplies of money (unlike at S. Croce) to build any of the horrendous suggestions, like that (**24**) designed in the 1830s.

Brunelleschi was sixty years old when in 1440, as the most famous and respected architect in Florence, he was asked to prepare plans for the new basilica of S. Spirito. He saw little of it built, dying in 1446 only a few days after the first column had been erected on the foundations. The architects who finished the building made various modifications to the exterior (which greatly annoyed Vasari despite his own cavalier modification of many Gothic churches in Tuscany for Cosimo I in the next century) but were careful to complete the interior largely as Brunelleschi had intended.

The interior looks its best if we stand in the middle of the near end of the nave. The arcade continues unbroken into the transepts to form a latin cross and unite the entire church, though the effect is partly spoiled by the seventeenth-century baldacchino in the crossing. The chapels around the walls sit in identical niches and are bathed,

like the rest of the church, in a dim grey light reflected from the pietra serena of the columns, arches and internal façades, creating an effect of extraordinary tranquillity and elegance.

If in S. Maria del Carmine the church is dull and the paintings stupendous then the opposite is true in S. Spirito, though a visitor in the seventeenth century would have found Raphael's *Madonna del Baldacchino*, and a Pontormo *Crucifixion* before they were sold off and added to the collections in the Pitti and the Uffizi. There are only one or two very good paintings—Filippino Lippi's *Madonna and Saints* with the patron and his wife in the bottom corners (second chapel from the left in the right transept) and an unusual *St Monica with Augustinian Nuns* (left chapel of the facing wall in the left transept) usually attributed to Botticini must be counted among them.

A chapel in the left nave leads into a delightful vestibule with a ceiling coffered in pietra dura; beyond it is an equally delightful octagonal sacristy. Both were designed by Giuliano da Sangallo and built in the last decade of the fifteenth century. A glass door at the end of the vestibule commands a tantalising but frustrating (as it is often locked) view across an early seventeenth-century cloister, where buildings in cream coloured plaster and pietra serena frame a blaze of plants and a dribbling fountain.

Turning left out of S. Spirito and walking on only a short distance, you arrive at the mid-point of Via Maggio. A little way to the left at the other side of the street is the Palazzo Firidolfi (No. 9) where Horace Walpole spent part of a cold winter in 1740. Like many other northern Europeans he was caught off guard by the severity of the Italian winter. Though at first delighted with his rooms on the *piano nobile*, he soon began to long for the snugness of a library in London and remarked with characteristic wit that as most of the walls were painted in fresco '. . . one has the additional horror of freezing with imaginary marble.' If we now turn our backs to the river and walk to the far end of Via Maggio we shall arrive at **Casa Guidi**, the last house on the right-hand side—hardly the most romantic house in Florence but nevertheless for more than a decade the home of two of the most famous English poets of their generation, Robert and Elizabeth Browning.

They could scarcely believe their ears when told, soon after their arrival in Florence in 1848 following a secret marriage in London, that eight enormous rooms on the first floor all furnished, according to Robert, 'as if for the Grand Duke' could be rented for only a guinea a week. They lived here for thirteen years until Elizabeth's death in 1861. In that time, inspired either by the stimulating views of the Pitti, home of the Austrian oppressors, from the windows of their apartment, or by copious draughts of heady Chianti, she became the most celebrated poet in Italy and the Casa Guidi a shrine visited by everyone from Swinburne to Risorgimento generals. Though the Brownings have come to symbolise the English in Italy in the mid-nineteenth century, they were regarded by their expatriate contemporaries as more than mildly eccentric. Elizabeth, six years older than Robert, dressed her son Penini (born in 1849, when she was 41) as a little girl and took a serious interest in spiritualism. Her most famous poem, three lines of which are inscribed on a marble plaque beneath her bedroom windows, was originally rejected by the editor of *Blackwood*'s Magazine who returned it with a note advising her to 'adorn the domestic circle in future'. Their apartment is now a Browning Museum (opening times, see p. 229; ring bell at Piazza S. Felice 2).

A short way up the Via Romana is La Speccola, a zoological museum worth a visit only to see the two unusually gruesome and macabre wax sculptures by Gaetano Zumbo, a Sicilian priest turned artist who for a short time worked for Cosimo III and his son. Depicting decay and death in a palette of lurid colours and with the help of real hair and bone, contrasting the beautiful with the repulsive, they are horrificably macabre and should on no account be missed.

Turning the other way, we come face to face with the Pitti Palace, which is the object of a separate visit (see next chapter). At the further end of the Piazza Pitti is the house where the great historian Francesco Guicciardini (1483–1540) wrote his classic *History of Italy*, but not behind the present façade, which was built in the 1920s. As you can see in Photograph **25**, the left side of

25

Via Guicciardini beyond did not exist at all for about five years after 1944 when it was pointlessly blown up to block the approaches to the Ponte Vecchio, though the river was dry and the Ponte Vecchio too weak to carry anything but light vehicles. The present buildings, like the new *borghi* overlooking the river, are the design of Giovanni Michelucci, an architect hailed by his admirers as 'Italy's Corbusier' and who was (for reasons not immediately obvious) judged the ideal architect for the difficult job of piecing together the ruins.

Turning left down the first side street Michelucci ends and medieval begins. It leads to a tiny piazza with no name but a pleasant café where we can sit outside and drink coffee. The view may not be much to write home about but what it lacks in spectacle this café makes up in atmosphere, for you sit at the nerve-centre of Florentine artisanry. Now and again as you sip your *cappuccino* the sweet smell of varnish or the heavy odour of oil paint may drift your way from one of the many workshops in the surrounding lanes. Occasionally the quiet will be interrupted by the whine of a drill, the chipping of a carpenter, or an artisan may lumber past on a bicycle balancing his weight against a regilded candlestick or a restuffed sofa. What are they all doing? Many are repairing antiques for foreign dealers, others are producing replicas to order or making anything from frames to bookshelves, others still are no doubt continuing a tradition that has been going strong in Florence ever since the eighteenth century—making fake antiques for rich foreigners. There is certainly no faking at Bertolino's extraordinary workshop at No. 5 Via dei Vellutini (the lane that leads from the south-west corner of the piazza) which is always open in working hours and definitely worth a visit.

Via Toscanella leads to the Borgo S. Jacopo where we turn right and walk to the end of the Ponte Vecchio (**26**), the three sturdy arches of which have resisted countless devastating floods but were not required to match their strength against dynamite in 1944 as it was spared from annihilation on the special orders of Hitler. It spans the Arno at its narrowest point and is probably the site of the original Roman bridge which

carried the traffic of the Via Cassia. The oldest parts of the present bridge date from 1345, but most of the shops are a century later and a distressingly large number of their most admired features result from a restoration in 1865. For visitors to Florence in the nineteenth century it was the place where the past seemed to come most happily alive. Wordsworth imagined Dante crossing it to meet Beatrice, others could picture the savage murder of Buondelmonte dei Buondelmonti in 1215 at the far end, which sparked off the Guelph-Ghibelline wars. Today its atmosphere and its occupants provide a less potent tonic to the imagination.

Much of the charm of the Ponte Vecchio derives from the superb aerial corridor linking the Pitti with the Uffizi, which was built by Vasari in the 1560s. It does some amusing acrobatics above our heads to skirt around the medieval Torre Manetti before leaping Via dei Bardi and crashing through a house on the far side of the road. It re-emerges around the corner (walk up Via Guicciardini and turn left) and shoots across the front of S. Felicità on an arcade, vastly improving its façade.

S. Felicità, which we must quickly visit, is possibly the oldest church in Florence, being founded in the late second or early third century. Sadly nothing remains of what was probably a fine early Christian interior. It has been rebuilt many times, most recently in the late 1730s (by a local architect called Ferdinando Ruggieri) in a strange but curiously successful style that, while absorbing the Florentine tradition, gives it a new life and a certain sparkle. He was adequately sensitive to leave standing all the sixteenth-century chapels and the seventeenth-century choir that had been added to the medieval church. These contain some superb paintings: the altarpiece of the Capponi Chapel (immediately to your right as you come in the door, light switch to left beside pilaster), the *Deposition* (1526) by Jacopo Pontormo, is one of the most remarkable and overtly emotional Mannerist paintings of the early sixteenth century. The limpid, drooping body of Christ lies perfectly still at a diagonal across the centre of the composition, surrounded and emphasised by a seething crowd of semi-androgynous figures in contorted poses and painted in glowing, semi-

Map 7
The Oltrarno (East)

1. Forte del Belvedere
2. Museo Bardini
3. S. Niccolò sopr' Arno
4. S. Miniato al Monte

PONTE ALLE GRAZIE

PIAZZA DEMIDOFF

COSTA S. GIORGIO

VIA DE' BARDI

PORTA S. MINIATO

PORTA S. NICOLÒ

S. NICOLÒ

PIAZZALE MICHELANGELO

TO ARCETRI

N

0   100   200 metres

200 yards

MUSEO BARDINI ✦ 141

luminous, almost ethereal colours. The *Annunciation* on the right side, also by Pontormo, was probably painted a year later. The tondoes in the vault are by Pontormo's pupil Agnolo Bronzino, though the older master may have had a hand in one of them.

* * *

The Piazza S. Felicità turns into Piazza de' Rossi, and from its right corner runs what is probably the most charming street in Florence, the Costa S. Giorgio. A balm to our various battered senses, it seems to lead up into an enchanted world scented by roses and jasmine and enlivened by surprise views into gardens full of olive and fig trees or across the Arno to the façade of the Uffizi. After about a hundred yards you pass the local church, S. Giorgio sulla Costa, which is rarely open, a pity as it has a good baroque interior by Foggini (1705). If we were to continue to the top of the Costa we would pass the house (on the left, No. 19) where Galileo spent some of his younger and freer days. A small way beyond it is the Porta S. Giorgio and the Forte del Belvedere, where there is usually an exhibition and always a superb view over

Florence. Some twenty minutes further on, along one of the most beautiful country roads in the world, is Arcetri (see page 214).

Otherwise turn left down the Costa della Scarpuccia. This leads to Via dei Bardi where George Eliot chose to house the heroine of *Romola*, her long, beautifully written but amazingly dull novel set in fifteenth-century Florence. It remains as tranquil and unspoilt as in the days when she came here for three hectic weeks to 'work up local colour', a task in which, reading the book today, we might be tempted to think she was somewhat overzealous.

If we turn right we will pass the finest surviving late medieval houses in the city before reaching the Piazza dei Mozzi at the far side of which stands the not very pretty Palazzo built in the 1880s by Stefano Bardini (1836–1922), an Italian Duveen who amassed a considerable fortune through dealing in and exporting works of art. He left his collection and the Palazzo to the state on his death and it is now open to the public (opening times, see p. 228). Though a visit to its enormous tomb-like rooms is a depressing experience not to be

142 ✤ PIAZZA DEMIDOFF

attempted if we feel in any way melancholy, it contains many fine things. Some of the most interesting are the architectural fragments that Bardini saved from the demolished wreckage of the Mercato Vecchio and some of the finest Persian carpets in Italy.

We have already walked a long way and whether or not we have opted to visit the Museo Bardini we will doubtless appreciate being able to turn left and sit down for a few minutes in the Piazza Demidoff which runs along the Lungarno. Here we can pass the time by contrasting the present views both across and up the Arno with those in Photographs **26** and **28**, and cannot fail to observe the many and perhaps not entirely happy changes that have occurred in Florentine topography over the last century. The Ponte alle Grazie which in Photograph **27** we see was a thirteenth-century bridge of great character with seven tiny shrines, one over every pier, each inhabited by a nun, was demolished in the 1890s though the present bridge is post-Second World War. Beyond it on the right is a deadbeat financial exchange which has replaced the charming old wool-dyeing factories seen in

Photograph **28**. Opposite is the less than delicate façade of the late nineteenth-century Biblioteca Nazionale. Nevertheless the spectacle remains impressive and without colossal melancholy we can now turn to the centre of the Piazza where, beneath an iron and glass umbrella, is the **Demidoff Monument** by Lorenzo Bartolini, the outstanding Italian sculptor of the mid-nineteenth century, who broke from the severe neo-classicism of Canova to a more naturalistic, romantic and occasionally (one must admit) more sentimental style easily distinguished from its many imitators during the second half of the century by his lightness and delicacy. Prince Niccolò Demidoff was a Russian who arrived in Florence as the Czar's ambassador to Tuscany in 1822. Reputed to be one of the richest men in Russia, his income of six million roubles a year when converted into Tuscan lire proved more than adequate to keep the wolf from the door. His entertainments far outshone those of the parsimonious but affable Grand Duke who was known to fine his servants for forgetting to turn out the gas lights in the Pitti.

27

Demidoff bought the Palazzo at the far end of the Piazza as well as the magnificent Medicean villa of Pratolino with a 150-acre garden designed by Buontalenti and set about collecting art and furniture with a purse so open that one can still almost imagine the fluttering pulses of the antique dealers whose services he required. Much loved in this quarter, he took a paternalistic interest in the welfare of its local residents, building them workhouses, schools and hospitals. History does not recall whether he behaved with equal charity to the armies of serfs who toiled away in his silver mines in the Urals and arms factories outside Petersburg. Like the Grand Dukes from Lorraine with whom they got on so well, the Demidoffs did not take long to become thoroughly Italianised. Niccolò's son Anatole settled in Florence and married Jerome Bonaparte's daughter.

From Palazzo Demidoff (now called Palazzo Serristori) a road to the right leads back to Via dei Bardi and, turning left, we arrive in a lively residential area. S. Niccolò sopr'Arno, on the Piazza, is a twelfth-century church with an attrac-tively classicised late sixteenth-century interior. It was in a second-hand furniture shop somewhere near here that in 1890 Bernard Berenson came across an exquisite altarpiece by the Sienese artist Sassetta which the shop owner was just about to cut up and make into boxes. He bought it for a few shillings and gave it pride of place at I Tatti, his villa near Settignano, where it provided him with a conversation piece for life. Paintings of such quality are rarely to be found in the antique shops of S. Niccolò today.

The Porta S. Niccolò, a few hundred yards further on, is the tallest and most impressive of the surviving gates and is now set in a dramatic piazza designed in the 1880s by Giuseppe Poggi. To the right is the Porta S. Miniato, and the path leading to the most lovable and memorable Florentine church—S. Miniato al Monte.

The walk from here to S. Miniato while not very long is steep and those who feel that they have already walked quite far enough should step into the closest café, drop a gettone into a telephone box and dial 4390 or 4798 for a taxi. If you wish to walk, the route is fairly obvious. About a hundred yards from the Porta S. Miniato we will reach a long, straight, uphill path which leads, past the Stations of the Cross, to the Viale. Here we turn right, cross the road and climb the flight of steps to the left, and we reach S. Miniato.

It is very difficult not to be impressed by or to like **S. Miniato al Monte**. Though stylistically entirely different, its appeal is comparable to that of the famous pilgrim's church at Vézelay in Burgundy. A purity and clarity radiates from the façade that cannot be attributed solely to the beauty of the green, white and black marbles from which it is built, or its simple, taut and clean inlaid geometrical decoration. It is very old indeed. The first foundations seem to have been dug in 1018. At that time Florence was still a very small and poor city and the limitations imposed on its builders by a shortage of resources are fairly obvious, both inside and out. Only the lower part of the façade was completed in the eleventh century. The upper, more complex incrustations (including the only classically 'impure' part of the façade, the simulated arcade inserted between the entablature and the pediment) were added in the twelfth century. Inside, only the columns and arches supporting the arcade, the columns and arches of the crypt and the decoration in the apse are contemporary with the building of the church. The choir and choir screens, altar, pulpit, floor, and the mosaics over the altar were all completed later, when Florence was beginning to become much richer.

The interior is no less impressive than the façade. It remains almost in its original state, while the additions that have been made in later centuries do nothing but add to its beauty. Even the brightly painted beams of the roof, and the *trompe l'oeil* arcades along the façades of the nave, all added in the late nineteenth century and usually referred to as 'a disastrous restoration', do little to disrupt the harmony of the design. There is much to see in the church. Where should we begin? Perhaps with the floor of the central aisle. The seven intarsiaed panels decorated with signs of the zodiac and animals are dated by some art historians to 1207 and are rather finer than the earliest parts of the Baptistery floor. Then glance at the frescoes on the right wall, the finest of which are, I think, at the near end, particularly the enormous *St Christopher* by an unknown fourteenth-century artist. At the far end of the nave stands the superb Cappella del Crocifisso erected in 1448 to the designs of Michelozzo. Though an elegant little structure in itself it is tactfully demure and makes every effort not to impose on its restrained surroundings. For its existence we have to thank, as so often in Florence, the Medici. For it was commissioned by Piero 'the Gouty', the faintly sinister figure who enjoyed a brief but effective interregnum between Cosimo il Vecchio and Lorenzo the Magnificent, to house a sacred Crucifix (now removed) that obligingly spoke to St John Gualberto. Like the more famous tabernacle in SS. Annunziata which was likewise commissioned by Piero from Michelozzo at almost the same time, this was the sort of publicly visible patronage, contributing to their prestige not just in Florence but in Rome, of which the Medici were particularly fond. The painted panels within the tabernacle are by Agnolo Gaddi, the fourteenth-century painter most famous for his work in S. Croce.

More delights await you in the raised choir. There is the pulpit with a superb lectern supported by an eagle perched on a saint who is himself perched on a lion. The mosaic above in the apse is late thirteenth century. It was made by artists brought from Ravenna and represents *Christ between the Virgin and S. Minias*, a Greek martyr whose head is said to have flown from the scaffold up the hill from Florence and come to rest on this site, thus leading to the foundation of the church. Some of the scenes from his life can be seen in an altarpiece to the right of the apse by a good early fourteenth-century artist called Jacopo del Casentino. The Sacristy to the right contains the over-restored frescoes of Spinello Aretino. After a visit to the crypt below and an appreciative glance at its fine and very early altar containing the relics of S. Minias, including, one imagines, his head, we can look at what is probably the most 'important' part of the church: the chapel of the Cardinal of Portugal (1461–6) in the left nave, a remarkable quintessence and amalgamation of everything most lovely in mid-fifteenth-century Tuscan art. Again the Medici are responsible for its existence. The

Cardinal was James of Lusitania, a young member of the Portuguese Royal Family who died aged 23 in Florence while on a diplomatic mission. The Medici, at their own expense but once again, no doubt, with an eye on their international reputation, honoured him with a private chapel. The architectural shell is by Manetti, Brunelleschi's most important pupil, and is a simplified and much smaller version of the Old Sacristy in San Lorenzo, and like it is decorated with the greatest sensitivity by Luca della Robbia whose ceramic ceiling gives the impression of spatial recession and thus makes the chapel appear larger than it is. On the left wall (looking in) is Alessio Baldovinetti's *Annunciation*, not an exceptional painting and one that would not stand out if hung, say, in the Uffizi but which has all the purity of line, the graceful, charming figures and the mellow colouring that characterise the finest painting of the period. Opposite lies the Cardinal himself. The tomb is by one of the best fifteenth-century sculptors then at the peak of his career, Antonio Rossellino. The chapel is a monument to the sophistication of contemporary Florentine culture.

Walking out of the church and looking at the view, it requires some imagination to picture Florence as it must have looked when S. Miniato was begun. There was, of course, no Duomo. On the northern bank of the river, within a large square of earth and rubble walls there must have been a densely packed, probably highly squalid few acres inhabited by ten or twenty thousand people and studded with several hundred pencil towers rising into the sky. For so small and relatively impoverished a city to contemplate the construction of so great a church, and to choose to build it not in the style of their neighbours but in that of the ancient Romans is no less remarkable than their achievements in later centuries.

Bus No. 14 from Piazzale Michelangelo will take you back into Florence. If, however, you now feel the allure of the Tuscan countryside, you are little more than a mile from Arcetri, where you can eat at the Trattoria Omero, that offers very good, if plain, Florentine cooking. To walk there continue on up the Viale for about five minutes, take the first left and from there on either follow signs or ask for directions.

FLORENCE OF THE GRAND DUKES: THE PALAZZO PITTI

✤ The **Palazzo Pitti** (opening times, see p. 230), while not the most ingratiating or subtle building in the world, has a certain rugged charm and suffers from no shortage of admirers. Even John Ruskin, who disapproved of almost everything built or decorated by the Medici Grand Dukes, saw something worthy of praise in its muscular façades and described it as 'brother heart to the mountain from which it is wrent'. But without question its most enthusiastic admirers were the Grand Dukes themselves to whom it gave enormous pleasure. As the last of them, Gian Gastone, lay on his death-bed his confessor attempted to allay his fears of the hereafter by reminding him of the beauties of paradise. 'But what could be more beautiful than the Pitti?' Gian Gastone is said to have replied before his final relapse.

But if the Pitti can be judged impressive, not everyone will think it beautiful and it seems ironic that the Medici, a family famous for their good taste, their inestimable contribution to the history of Western art and their immense wealth, should have lived in what must be one of the least elegant palaces in Europe. It happened largely by accident: what you see now is the result of three centuries of piecemeal addition. The original palazzo was built by the Pitti family in the mid-fifteenth century and comprises only the seven

BELVEDER CON PITTI

29

windows at the centre of the present façade. (29) Cosimo I and his rich Spanish wife Eleonora of Toledo bought it in 1549, but as what had been an imposing mansion for a fifteenth-century banker was clearly insufficiently grand for a sixteenth-century prince, they added two wings that stretch into the Boboli Gardens. In the 1630s their great-grandson Ferdinando II toyed with the idea of lowering the level of the Piazza and adding a swirling baroque staircase up to the ground floor but, perhaps sensibly, opted simply to extend the existing façade. (30) The two *Rondi* enclosing the Piazza were built in the late eighteenth and early nineteenth centuries by the Dukes of Lorraine, who succeeded to Tuscany at the death of the last male Medici in 1737 and ruled, with an extended break during the Napoleonic wars, unil the collapse of Austrian power in Italy obliged them to abdicate in 1859.

However off-putting its façade, the Pitti is captivating within. Like Versailles, though on a smaller scale, it evokes the stiff, gilded magnificence of a seventeenth-century court, and is the true mausoleum to a long extinct but peculiarly intriguing dynasty of princes. It retains most of its original furniture, paintings and decoration, largely through the admirable will of the last of the Medici, Anna Maria, the Electress Palatine. On her death in 1743 she left the entire Medicean patrimony, the greatest princely art collection in the world, to the people of Florence, stipulating that 'these things, being for the ornament of the state, the benefit of the people and for an inducement to the curiosity of foreigners, nothing shall be alienated or taken away from the capital or territories of the Grand Duchy'. It now contains five different museums.

Walking through the entrance, we enter Ammanati's superb courtyard, one of the most impressive examples of Italian late sixteenth-century Mannerist architecture. Calculated to create an effect of regal splendour, two vast rusticated stone wings (built in 1558–70) frame a fountain where putti pirouette in a white spray of water. Behind them rises the steep, shadowy blur of the Boboli which, through tricks of perspective, seems to stretch far into the distance and up to the Forte del Belvedere.

As the Pitti had to accommodate not just the

VEDVTA DELLA PIAZZA DEL REAL PALAZZO DE PITTI, NEL TEMPO CHE VI FV POSATA LA MIRACOLOSA IMMAGINE DI MARIA VERGINE DELL' IMPRVNETA IL DI XXII DI MAGGIO MDCCXI.

1. Clero di S Frediano, 2. Clero di S Piero Mag. 3 Clero di S Lorenzo, 4 Cherici e Cappellani della Metropolitana, 5 Canonici Fiorentini, 6 Mon.S Arcivescovo, 7 Il Piovano dell'Impruneta, 8 S.A Reale, 9 Il Ser. Principe Gio Gastone, 10 Cariche Maggiori, e Signori della Corte, 11 Luogotenente, 12 Il Podestà 13
14 Consiglieri Senatori con 15 Auditori di Ruota, 16 Il Console dell Accademia Fiorentina, 17 Il Proposto de Collegi, 18 Il Proposto de Procuratori di Palazzo, 19 e gli altri Magistrati, 20 Ser. Principe di Toscana, 21 Confessore di S.A. 22 Ser. Principessa di Toscana, 23 Ser. Principessa Elenora, 24 Dame della 25 Guardia del Corpo

Grand Duke but his relations and their families, its interior was, and to an extent still is, a labyrinth of different apartments. The right wing was reserved for foreigners and important guests, while the Medici themselves seem to have lived in that to the left. On its second floor are the rooms where Anna Maria (**31**), the last of the Medici, spent the last eighteen years of her pathetically wretched life in a solitary splendour described by Thomas Gray and Horace Walpole who, while travelling together as young men on the Grand Tour in 1741, were granted the rare privilege of an audience. They both describe a short woman, dressed entirely in black and wearing a veil, who stood in the middle of a room filled with silver furniture 'more magnificent than beautiful', and never smiled.

Though the Dukes of Lorraine began to break the terms of the will very soon after her death by selling jewellery and furniture, the major part of the collection remains intact. The one part of the Medicean legacy for which they showed an impeccable respect was the magnificent collection of old master paintings, mainly of the sixteenth century,

31

which they not only held together but augmented. The greater part of the collection, still in their original gilt frames and arranged, as with all seventeenth-century private galleries, more from the point of view of interior decoration than to provide a good view of the paintings, hang in the **Galleria Palatina** (open as for Palazzo Pitti), a magnificent set of rooms on the first floor.

Climb the great stone staircase (after buying tickets on the ground floor). As you rise to the first-floor landing a glittering perspective opens before your eyes down the enfilade through rooms hung with chandeliers and scattered with antique sculpture. Two fine portraits of the last Medicean males, Gian Gastone (left), whose hand rests on a diamond-studded crown, and opposite, his rather more distinguished brother Ferdinando wrapped in ermine, provide a suitable overture to the grand opera that lies before us.

To enter the Galleria Palatina is to be swept in an instant to the Medici court in the seventeenth century. The Sala di Venere is the first and grandest of five marvellous baroque rooms painted in the 1640s by Pietro da Cortona and his assistants. The most sought-after Italian painter of his day, his reputation was based upon his stupendous ceiling in the Galleria of the Palazzo Barberini in Rome. The scheme of decoration, conceived around the type of complex allegory fashionable in the seventeenth century, where each room is dedicated to a planet which is in itself symbolic of a princely virtue, is really a convenient excuse for the Medici to wax lyrical on their favourite obsession—the grandeur and importance both of their ancestors and of their dynastic connections. Through the marriage of Francesco I's daughter Marie de Medici to Henry IV of France and of her daughters to Charles I of England and Philip IV of Spain, they could claim a close blood-tie with the three most important royal houses in Europe, and this went badly to their heads.

As in the estimation of all but themselves they were but one among many Italian princely families, there is a temptation to react against this kind of Medicean *folie de grandeur*, and most of their historians have. Their splendour and glory was 'but as the phosphorescent light that may be seen to float above the putrescent remains of organic matter in the process of dissolution' said Anthony Trollope in his *History of Florence* of 1865. Mark Twain called Cosimo I and his successors 'the dead and damned Medici who cruelly tyrannised over Florence and were her curse for over two hundred years', though for the most part they were enlightened, intelligent despots. 'To revere them,' wrote the Earl of Cork more sensibly in 1755 'you must consider their generosity, their benefactions, their policy and their scientific institutions. To view them with horror you need only listen to the undoubted outrages of their private lives.' In fact the only Grand Duke whose life can really be called outrageous was the last— Gian Gastone (1671–1737). **(32)** He is supposed to have left the Pitti only once in his last ten years and on that occasion was violently and publicly sick out of the window of his carriage.

Intelligent if sometimes indolent, bored by government if fascinated by the opulent, elegant or the unusual, the Medici lived in an atmosphere of formality and luxury that is not easy to picture today—eating off gold plate in rooms hung with

32

Titians and Raphaels and employing a corps of chairmen to carry them even up and down stairs (their dislike of all forms of physical exercise may explain their unnatural longevity, two of the Grand Dukes reigned for about fifty years). Until the end of the seventeenth century, with the exception of the occasional black sheep, they remained the model of cultivated princes, patronising and protecting Galileo, who repaid them by naming the four moons around Saturn the *Stelle Medicee*, collecting paintings and sculpture and encouraging science. Gian Gastone's brother, the Crown Prince Ferdinando, was the greatest Italian patron of his age, commissioned operas from Scarlatti and collected some of the best pictures in this gallery. Other Medicean cardinals and Princes bought paintings while travelling through Europe and persuaded artists from Spain, the Low Countries and France to visit Tuscany. As a result the Palatina is one of the most delightfully varied galleries in Europe, though chronologically its range is quite narrow.

Standing in the centre of the Sala di Venere is Canova's *Venus*, unveiled to universal admiration in 1812. Commissioned in 1803 to replace the Venus de' Medici taken to Paris by Napoleon (along with six Titians, four Raphaels and an Andrea del Sarto amongst other things) from the Venetian Antonio Canova, then considered the greatest Italian sculptor since Michelangelo, it makes many departures from the original. Taller than the Venus de' Medici, she has a slight stoop, so avoiding the impression (so obvious in the original) that the head is too large for the body, and clutches a piece of drapery to her bosom thus introducing that quality of shy modesty that the nineteenth century found so alluring. Canova called her 'a Venus of his own creation' and she became one of the most popular of his works.

The first two paintings that catch the eye are both by Titian and hang on the right wall. His famous *La Bella* (1536, to the left) and that of his friend the cynic and wit *Pietro Aretino* (1545). These arrived in Florence, along with many other great paintings, on the marriage of Ferdinand II to the Urbino heiress Vittoria della Rovere in 1638. **(33, 34)** In both one is struck by the opulence of colour and the quality of detail. Gold and silver

34

threads are picked out in *La Bella*'s lace trimming, rubies and emeralds are set into her hair band. The wrinkles and warts on his face were all too realistic for Aretino, who called the painting a 'hideous marvel', refused to hang it in his house and gladly presented it to Cosimo I.

Above them is a powerful maritime scene by Salvator Rosa (1615–73), the brilliant, if unpredictable, Neapolitan heavily patronised by the Medici through most of the 1640s. Here we see him in a romantic mood. In the background cliffs tumble into the waves, while the sky is an angry blue that threatens a storm. If powerful, it has none of the strangely macabre and sinister qualities of his self-portrait (left wall to right of door) called *La Menzogna* (c.1651) as a penitent contemplating his death mask in the flickering light of a single candle. It would be difficult to realise, looking at the quality of Rubens' pair of glowing, Brueghelesque pastoral scenes (c.1637) to either side of the entrance door, that they were painted at the very end of his life when he was barely able to move his fingers through chronic gout and his left arm was half-paralysed with arthritis.

Immediately to the right of the door in the next room, the Sala di Apollo, is a large *Cleopatra* clutching a comically minuscule serpent by Guido Reni (1575–1642) the Bolognese artist who worked mainly in Florence. To the left of the entrance wall is Van Dyck's *Charles and Henrietta Maria*. Laden with hints at the sitters' characters, painted with an almost photographic precision (particularly the lace on the Queen's dress), this is just one of many superb examples of Van Dyck's portraiture. To the right of the door is perhaps the most lovely of the many paintings by the artist who for Henry James set the tone of the entire gallery and whose work looks most comfortable amongst its decorative splendour— the *Holy Family* by Andrea del Sarto, the most important Florentine high Renaissance artist.

On the facing wall is another pair of portraits by Titian. On the left is one of his most popular paintings, frequently repeated and copied for different patrons, a lush *Penitent Magdalene* (1531), seductively naked with hair cascading over her bosom. To the right hangs one of the great portraits of the sixteenth century—the *Grey-Eyed*

Nobleman (1541), sometimes called the Englishman—a quintessent image of the romantic aristocrat.

Two very different paintings by Rubens dominate the Sala di Marte, the next room. The enormous *Consequences of War* (1638) was a generous gift from the painter to Justus Sustermans, his fellow-countryman employed for most of his life as court painter to the Medici. Its remarkable energy is achieved partly by the power of the composition, which is based on the line running upward from the great bare leg of Venus through her arms (as she tries to restrain Mars from destroying the world) and up into a demon holding a burning torch. Other figures and scenes such as the destruction of *Prosperity*, *Art* and *Civilisation* accentuate the same movement.

Rubens (second from left) sits with his brother and their two closest friends in the studiedly calm and tranquil *Four Philosophers*, a painting that provides a reminder that, apart from being one of the most productive painters in the history of art, Rubens was an accomplished diplomat and scholar. They sit below an antique bust, supposedly of Seneca, one of Rubens' most treasured possessions, and the eye is caught by those meticulous still-life details in which he excels.

In the centre of the entrance wall is one of the best-known paintings by Van Dyck, Rubens' greatest pupil, of *Cardinal Bentivoglio* (c.1623), the Papal ambassador to the Low Countries and then to France. Though confined by the conventions of official portraiture, Van Dyck manages to convey a remarkable sense of the sitter's character. Covered in warm crimson and icy lace, his long, thin fingers holding a document, sitting straight on an opulently upholstered chair, he personifies the shrewd, worldly, yet dignified prince of the Church.

Ippolito de' Medici (1532, right wall), a grandson of Lorenzo the Magnificent, was the only member of the Medici to be painted by Titian. A romantic if mysterious figure, here he is dressed as a Hungarian noble to celebrate his role in a successful defence of Vienna against the Turks. His life might have been long and colourful had he not fallen victim to Renaissance intrigue and been poisoned three years after sitting for this portrait.

On the facing wall of the Sala di Giove is Raphael's exquisite *Donna Velata* (1516) in which the minutely detailed sleeve covered in gold threads and emeralds contrasts with the simpler treatment of the subject's face and hair. On the window wall is a small *Portrait of a Youth* by Carlo Dolci (1616–86) who, though largely ignored today, was in the middle years of the seventeenth century the most famous Florentine, probably Italian, artist, and his work was particularly popular with English collectors. Though he was known to spend a whole week painting only a few square inches of canvas, and months on a foot or a hand, he nevertheless produced a great quantity of work, much of which is to be seen in the Palatina and in the Galleria of the Palazzo Corsini.

The Sala di Saturno, next door, is also liberally endowed with old masters and is particularly rich in the work of Raphael. There is perhaps no room in the world where we can better appreciate the extraordinary artistic development of that artist. He arrived in Florence in 1498 as a young man still far from sure of his own style. Within twenty years he was the most fashionable painter in Europe,

living in his own palazzo staffed by a retinue of servants and employing a small army of assistants in order to cope with a deluge of Papal and royal commissions. The portraits on the right wall of *Agnolo and Maddalena Doni* (c.1505–6, the same couple that commissioned the *Holy Family* by Michelangelo in the Uffizi) are thought to be the first important paintings of his Florentine period. His style is clearly based on that of Leonardo da Vinci, who had only recently left Florence for France. The backgrounds, Maddalena's coy smile, and the quality of the light all remind one of Leonardo's great Madonnas, though there is just as clearly a trace of his first master, Perugino. The first of the two ecclesiastical portraits—of *Cardinal Bibbiena* (1511)—reveals a growing self-confidence, though it is only with his *Cardinal Inghirami* (1516) and more importantly the *Madonna della Seggiola* (1515), that you see the fully mature artist. The latter is perhaps the best known, best liked and most often imitated of all Raphael's paintings—in the middle of the nineteenth century there was a five-year waiting list of artists wishing to paint copies. It takes a well known and traditional theme and revolution-ises it. Christ, usually placed asymmetrically in the tondo, is put at its centre and the composition 'spins' from his elbow. 'Let the eye travel from the centre, the child's elbow,' wrote Jacob Burck-hardt, 'and follow the light as it spreads through the picture. The charm is the relationship be-tween the draped and the undraped parts, the unrestrained flow of lines.' (Raphael's great portrait of Leo X with two Cardinals hangs in the Uffizi.)

The decoration of the large Sala dell' Iliade next door was intended by Pietro da Cortona to be the climax in his sequence of rooms, but he died before he could execute his ideas. The present ceiling (1819–20), by Luigi Sabatelli, is much admired by cognoscenti of neo-classicism. On the window wall is a fine but anonymous portrait of *Elizabeth I* (an unusual subject for the gallery of a Catholic prince since she was a Protestant and the principal foe of Tuscany's closest ally, the King of Spain) looking like the shimmering ice queen from the frozen north.

The portraits of Justus Sustermans (1597–1681),

court painter to the Medici for over forty years, are usually ignored in Florence just because they are so numerous. Nevertheless, they are of great quality. Without absurdly flattering his far from attractive subjects, he compensates for their lack of looks by endowing them with a certain grandeur and nobility. A case in point is his portrait of the middle-aged and corpulent *Prince Mattias* (entrance wall), the most entertainingly dissolute of the Medici, who, when dressed in a swirling satin cape and half concealed in a cavalier's hat stuffed with ostrich plumes, looks almost majestic. The same problems do not apply in the portrait of the young, good-looking *Waldemar, Prince of Denmark* (facing wall), one of his best-known paintings.

From here we must look quickly at the small but delightful Room 26, the Sala della Stufa (reached by taking the further door on the right of the Sala dell' Iliade). The frescoes on the walls, representing *The Four Ages of the World*, were painted by Pietro da Cortona (between 1637 and 1641). It proved such a success that on the strength of it he was commissioned to paint the entire

35

gallery. In Room 25, to the right, is the *Sleeping Cupid* attributed to Caravaggio, who worked little in Florence but died on Tuscan soil at Porto Ercole in the Monte Argentario, a chilling *Judith with the Head of Holofernes* by Cristofano Allori, a late Florentine painter, and several good Carlo Dolcis. The rooms beyond are as interesting for their decoration as for their paintings. The finest surviving examples of the Italian Empire style (which tends to be more refined and delicate than French Empire) they were decorated for Elisa Bacciochi, **(35)** Napoleon's able and cultivated sister, in her brief reign as mistress of the Pitti between 1809 and 1814 when Tuscany, under direct French rule, had become the Département de l'Arno. Elegant and adequately luxurious for one who considered herself 'de seconde en la Génie de la famille Impériale', she had the plans approved by the imperial architects Percier and Fontaine before beginning work. The bathroom (Room 24) to the left of the corridor is an example of neo-classical decoration at its most charming. If we walk through the next room with its small but lovely Filippino Lippi panel over the fireplace, and then the next which contains Filippo Lippi's magnificent *Madonna and Child* in tondo and Rubens' monochrome *Three Graces*, then on through a corridor, you arrive in the Sala della Musica, the happiest consequence of her redecorations.

Its magnificent ceilings and stucco wall decorations have survived intact, so has the original furniture—the drum-shaped commodes and a writing desk which ingeniously turns into a table. When the Dukes of Lorraine returned to Florence in 1814 they sensibly completed most of Elisa Bacciochi's decorative programme, though they effaced murals with such typically subtle Napoleonic themes as the *Glories of France* and the *Repose of Hercules* on the ceiling of the Imperial bedchamber.

The next room with its magnificent *pietra dura* table brings you to the end of the Galleria Palatina. Walking back on to the landing and turning to the right we arrive again at the beginning of the state apartments which occupy the other half of the enfilade and most of the southern wing of the Pitti.

*   *   *

The most enjoyable way to see the **State Apartments** is to look at little in particular and instead allow your imagination to evoke Viscontian images of the balls held here during the nineteenth century. The Grand Dukes would hold open house for Florentines and foreigners of rank or distinction once a week throughout the social season. At some point in the evening the Grand Duke and Grand Duchess would make an appearance and politely converse with their guests. In 1836 Ferdinand III was unlucky enough to engage James Fenimore Cooper, the verbose author of *The Last of the Mohicans*, on democracy—a touchy subject since Tuscany had none. From 1865 to 1870, when Florence was capital of Italy, the Pitti became the home of a new dynasty—the Kings of Savoy who had become, five years earlier, the Kings of a united Italy. Under the flamboyant Vittorio Emmanuele II the parties were even more lavish and one can almost imagine these rooms filled by the melodies of Verdi and Rossini, tables groaning with pistaccio puddings and sugar jellies, gorgeous women in crêpe de chine and flashing diamonds waltzing with men dressed in splendid Piedmontese uniforms. Though now probably filled with slightly less glamorous people, the rooms look very much as they did in 1870.

Some comment on a few among the many things which may catch your attention: the superb Gobelins tapestries in Room I were ordered from Paris by Elisa Bacciochi. She was disappointed when they arrived and wrote a furious note to the Minister of Culture in Paris saying that they were 'hardly worth the cost of transport' and 'of a lower quality that those which we keep in our furniture store'. They represent the *Triomphes des Dieux*, and whatever her objections may have been, to me they seem a consummate example of the art. Set in the fabulous East, the scenes are sprinkled with objets de luxe—caskets brimming over with pearls, jewels as big as ostrich eggs, dervishes, sultans and negroes, all meticulously picked out in gold and silver thread. Most of the furniture is seventeenth- and eighteenth-century. The best pieces tend to be from the princely collections of Parma, Lucca and Modena which were 'centralised' (meaning looted) after the unification of Italy.

Room III, the Sala del Trono, is the only one to have been entirely refurbished by the House of Savoy, and provides a characteristic example of their unerringly vulgar taste (seen at its most extreme in the Villa La Petraia). It was in here, on 9th October 1870, that Vittorio Emmanuele received the news of the Roman plebiscite uniting Italy and causing the capital to be moved from Florence to Rome. Room IV contains two splendid portraits by Sustermans. Room VI, with some surviving seventeenth-century ceiling decoration above the bed, is the only one to give any idea of how the Pitti looked under the Medici. At the far end of the enfilade, the circular Room IX is a rare example of Italian eighteenth-century chinoiserie.

Returning to the staircase landing, we are now faced with a choice. Do we wish to see another gallery or to walk into the Boboli Gardens and have a cup of coffee? If the former then we can walk upstairs to the **Galleria dell'Arte Moderna** (opening times, p. 230). It contains a large, varied collection mainly of nineteenth-century Italian paintings, including many by the 'Macchiaioli', the so-called 'Tuscan Impressionists', and late romantic paintings with amusing subjects such as Brunelleschi pondering over an egg and Dante contemplating the Inferno. Once these rooms contained the Grand Ducal library but in 1919 it was moved to the Biblioteca Nazionale and stored in the basement, only to be largely destroyed in the flood of 1966.

If walking into the gardens suits your mood better, then go down the stairs, turn right into the portico and follow the signs to the Boboli. The gardens are linked to the courtyard by a curving ramp at the top of which we might pause to admire a justly famous view over a red wash of tiled roofs to the Duomo, campanile and Fiesole in the far distance. The **Boboli** is the grandest of Tuscan gardens: the seventeenth-century amphitheatre in which we stand is the centrepiece of an impressive formal layout of clipped ilex and bay, of avenues, grottoes and an apparently infinite number of statues. Unfortunately it is also the steepest. A quotation from that eloquent millionaire dilettante William Beckford may encourage us to climb the hill and see a little more of it. In 1780 (when only 22) he arrived at the point where we

now stand after (he says with some exaggeration) descending '. . . alley after alley, bank after bank' from the top of the garden which '. . . brought the scenery of antiquity . . . so vividly to mind that . . . lost in a trail of recollections that this incident excited, I expected every instant to be called to dine at the table of Lucullus hard by . . . and to stretch myself on his purple trichinias.' You will find a café (closed in winter) by turning left at the top of the amphitheatre and walking on another fifty metres to a small green-roofed building, built in the 1770s as a pleasure pavillion. Although it can by no stretch of the imagination be compared to the table of Lucullus, here we can order coffee and admire the view from its windows out across the city and the Val d'Arno.

Although Florence has lost her medieval walls and gained the suburbs in the far distance since this pavillion was built, the view remains remarkably unspoilt. It is still the city of '. . . domes and spires occupying the vale' surrounded by '. . . green valleys of mountains occupied by villas, a Babylon of palaces and gardens' described by Shelley in the early nineteenth century. The 'Babylon of palaces and gardens' was built and laid out between the fifteenth and the eighteenth century by families of the Florentine aristocracy, the descendants of which, being occasionally a little short of money, have for the last century or two been forced to let them to wealthy foreigners sensible enough to make Florence their home. 'Most of them [the villas]', wrote Henry James in 1877, 'are offered for rent (many of them for sale) at prices unnaturally low: you may have a tower and a garden, a chapel and an expanse of thirty windows, for five hundred dollars a year.' The rents today are rather higher.

Far across to the right you can just see Fiesole, and just beneath it you may be able to make out the Villa Medici. Built by the younger son of Cosimo il Vecchio in the 1470s and surrounded by a wonderful garden, it is probably the most beautiful of the Medicean villas around Florence. It has been lived in by a succession of interesting and eccentric people—in the 1870s Holman Hunt used its stables as his studio. His landlord, William Blundell Spence, was an affluent *marchand amateur* in Florentine art, who discovered Botti-

celli's *Pallas and the Centaur* in a back passage of the Pitti shortly before he died in 1900. It was also the childhood home of Iris Origo, the most distinguished Anglo-Italian writer of the last fifty years (whose autobiography *Images and Shadows* is essential reading for anyone interested in the Anglo-Florentine community at its peak before and after the First World War).

The *Kaffeehaus*, as this pavillion always seems to have been known, was built by the second Habsburg/Lorraine Grand Duke, Pietro Leopoldo I (1765–90) who has been described as the most enlightened European ruler (**36**) of the late eighteenth century. Soon after his accession on the death of his father Francis Stephen (1737–65) he made Florence his home, dispensed with the regent and took an active interest in the welfare of his state. Like his more famous brother the 'musical' Emperor Joseph II, he was deeply affected by the ideas of the Enlightenment, and with some success attempted to improve the quality of life through positive legislation, abolishing the death penalty, making efforts to improve agriculture and encourage trade and by curbing the power of the

36

Church. He also, unlike his father, learnt Italian and opened the Boboli Gardens to the public.

It was largely due to Leopold's efforts that by the end of the eighteenth century Florence had become famous all over Europe as a peaceful, tolerant, and civilised place to live and had attracted a largish community of foreign residents. Its reputation increased after the Napoleonic wars and by the middle of the nineteenth century it had become, according to Alexandre Dumas '. . . like Venice at the time of Candide, the home of exiled Kings, of Russian princes covered in rivers of turquoises and torrents of emeralds . . . and the English of all ages, colours and rank'. On three afternoons a week the gardens were open to the public. The Piazza in front of the Pitti would be a crush of carriages and the Boboli full of ladies in crinoline and bonnets, accompanied by men in grey top hats and frock coats or by Austrian officers in their white uniforms. The subtleties and snobberies of Florentine social life in the mid-nineteenth century are admirably conveyed in a little book called *Life in Tuscany* written in 1859 by one Mabel Crawford. It is full of indispensable tips for the newly arrived expatriate who is advised not to visit the Boboli on Sunday afternoons 'unless' she says 'one wants to encounter one's maid or Italians of the lower social orders.'

If it is a Tuesday, Thursday or Saturday we can now visit the most enchanting part of the Boboli — the secluded **Giardino del Cavaliere** (opening times, p. 230) poised on the fortifications built by Michelangelo in 1527. Cool even on the most stifling summer days, with an enchanting view across rolling hills and to the Torre del Gallo in Arcetri, this is a place where we can avoid the heat and the crowds even in the height of the tourist season. Cosimo III (1642–1723) built the casino at one end and laid out the garden where he grew spices specially ordered from Java and Goa. The view remains much as it must have looked at the end of the seventeenth century. The landscape is still made up of those washed out olive greens and dark patches of cypress, faded yellows, brown walls and ordered rows of vines. Far to the left is the Forte del Belvedere and to the right stretch the city walls, covered in wild flowers and ivy.

The casino now contains a **Museum of**

Porcelain, not the 'soft paste' porcelain made, for the first time in Europe, in sixteenth-century Florence by Bernardo Buontalenti (which is now rare and hugely expensive though there are some examples in the Bargello), but the exquisite dinner services and candelabra made by the factories at Meissen, Sèvres, in Vienna and near Florence by the Ginori at Doccia (where there is another museum) from the end of the eighteenth century. The finest of its contents is perhaps the dinner service ordered from Sèvres by Elisa Bacciochi (on the centre table in the first room), though to some the most appealing of its contents must be the ceramic portrait of Napoleon above the fireplace, again commissioned by Elisa Bacciochi as a suitably Francophile decoration for her refurbished palazzo.

Cosimo III probably came up to the Giardino del Cavaliere in the evenings to drink lemonade and eat iced watermelon in the refreshing breeze, but throughout the day in July and August he could have been found in the summer apartments of the Pitti. These are not the light, airy rooms that you might imagine but vast and dark halls with thirty-foot-high ceilings and small, shuttered windows. They are of particular interest as they were beautifully painted just before and just after the rooms of the Galleria Palatina and in a style hardly less grand. They are now part of the **Museo degli Argenti** (opening times, p. 230) containing a collection of jewellery and decorative arts, and entered from the courtyard of the Pitti.

Take the path to the left of the Giardino del Cavaliere. This means a short detour in the descent through the gardens but will also allow us at least a glimpse of the most dramatic corner of the Boboli Gardens—the *Isolotto* designed by Alfonso Parigi in the 1630s. A marine fantasy of prancing horses and Sea Gods set in a pool of reflecting water, it lies at the end of the Viottolone, a grand avenue of columnar cypresses that march down the hill (between dense thickets that were planted not for the sake of art but of culinary delight, they are elaborate traps for birds that could be consumed at the grand-ducal table). Though on an impressive scale, from here it looks no more than a tantalising silver blur.

The path continues down this side of the hill

and comes out in front of La Meridiana, a harmless if slightly dull addition made to the Pitti by Pietro Leopoldo in the 1780s as the living quarters of his own family (it is now a **Museum of Clothes**, opening times, p. 230). Turn right here and fifty metres further on you find yourself back in front of the Pitti. The ramp leads down to the courtyard— the entrance to the **Museo degli Argenti** in the original Medici **Summer Apartments** is in the right-hand corner. (The entry fee is covered by the tickets to the Galleria Palatina.)

The first room contains some good late seventeenth-century Flemish tapestries and a family tree that may help unravel some of the confusions that inevitably result when a dynasty uses and reuses a very small number of names. It leads into a large and exceptionally grand room—the Sala di Giovanni da S. Giovanni, named after the artist commissioned to paint it on the marriage of Ferdinand II to Vittoria della Rovere in 1634. He died only two years after beginning, but by then had managed to complete the ceiling and right-hand wall. The other walls were painted by his pupils. Set in a rather ponderous architectural frame, they have none of the lightness or the subtlety of Pietro da Cortona's Sala della Stufa upstairs, painted only a year or two later.

Apart from the ceiling, which shows the happy pair betrothed, the paintings are an elaborate tribute to Lorenzo the Magnificent, some of whose treasure is displayed in the room to the left. His sixteen crystal and stone vases, most of them antique, some of them Byzantine, were collected throughout his life. It was objects like this— small, delicate, infinitely refined and made of exquisite materials—that interested Lorenzo more than paintings or sculpture by contemporary artists. He spent a large proportion of his ever-declining fortunes on jewels and antiques, though two years after his death the collection was tragically dispersed across Italy on the expulsion of the Medici from Florence. Many pieces were retrieved by Clement VII who used them for storing precious holy relics of eastern saints. It gives some insight into the confidence—or perhaps to the insensitivity—of Lorenzo and his age that he had his initials, LAU MED, cut in deep Roman letters into every vase.

At the other side of the Sala di Giovanni da S. Giovanni are three of the most delightful rooms in Florence. They were painted by two Bolognese artists famous throughout Europe as masters of *trompe l'oeil* — Agostino Michele and Agnolo Colonna — between 1636 and 1641. Using all sorts of perspective tricks and an architectural imagination fifty years in advance of their generation, they blur the divide between reality and fantasy. Colonnades of jade and blood-red granite rise into the clouds, cool marble terraces stretch into the far distance, spiral staircases rise to imaginary mezzanines and the whole charming, musical, magical world is lent a touch of wit by its population of comic figures. In the first room, which was used as an audience chamber, a small boy creeps up behind a balustrade to catch an escaped monkey. In the rather smaller second room a boy plays with a parrot, while another looks into the real piazza outside with his telescope through a false window, and at the other side of the room an absurdly overdressed courtier ascends a flight of steps. These irreverent touches must have provided the Medici with at least some diversion through the long, hot days of the Florentine summer.

The rooms to the right contain an amazing collection of virtuoso objects — examples of a branch of court art which was to find its ultimate expression in the nineteenth century with the work of Fabergé. Wonderfully mad, fabulously expensive, made from gold, silver and precious stones, products of fantasy intended to have no more important function than to look beautiful, they reveal not only the skills of their makers but the tastes and minds of the men whose lives they were intended to adorn — the later Medici, who took just as great a pride in them as in their collection of old masters. Nothing in the Pitti has quite the same power to bring to life the splendour and extravagance of their court as the sixteenth century vase in lapis lazuli finished in gold by Bernardo Buontalenti, or the incredible set of turned ivories by the German craftsman Balthazar Stockamer, which as pieces of virtuoso craftsmanship can have few rivals. With an inventiveness and delicacy that can match anything by Cellini, they balance on toppling columns of coins, and burst into sprays of tiny roses as if the material were as malleable as putty.

In the room to the right at the top of the stairs remains what was, on Anna Maria, the Electress Palatine's, death in 1743, one of the greatest collections of jewellery in Europe. Valued at four and a half million scudi, the Medicean jewels were worth only slightly less than the annual income of the state. Their inventories describe huge stones in appropriately gargantuan settings and ropes of pearls that might not have disgraced Dumas' Russians. Their value sealed their fate. Within two years of Anna Maria's death, despite the terms of her will, they had all gone into the melting pot to help Francis Stephen and Maria Theresa fight their endless wars with Frederick the Great for control of Silesia. The only objects to survive were those thought too unimportant to sell. These were kept in the Vienna Kunsthistorisches Museum and returned here in 1919 after the Peace of Versailles. The last Habsburg Emperor, Charles I, took the famous Medici diamond with him into exile and his son sold it on the Amsterdam diamond exchange in the 1930s. Despite these sad deple-

tions some fine objects remain in the collection, such as the two inlaid reliefs of *Cosimo I in Prayer* and *Cosimo II and his Family*.

In the rooms at the other side of the stairs are the treasures of the Archbishop of Salzburg, which with truly Habsburgian complexity came to be owned by Ferdinand III. With the exception of the silver gilt dishes in the first room they are mainly eccentric curiosities, like the chalice made from ostrich eggs and cups made from buffalo horns. Beyond this is a pretty painted room filled with ceramics—the most interesting things here are the four large pre-Columbian Mexican vases that found their way into the collection at the end of the seventeenth century. The terracotta plates are casts of the Medicean plate melted down in the 1770s. Beyond them the stairs lead back down to the ground floor.

No visit to the Pitti can be complete without a sight of its most hideous statue (immediately to your left as we enter the Boboli from the left-hand side of the palazzo)—Valerio Cioli's cruelly unflattering portrait of Cosimo I's obese court dwarf astride a turtle. Always known by its derogatory nickname of 'the Bacchus', it mocks not just the dwarf, with its lingering study of his physical repulsion and his inability to stretch his legs across the back of the turtle, but in its pose and expression it laughs at Ammanati's gargantuan and faintly pompous *Neptune* in the Piazza della Signoria, which had been finished only a few years earlier.

Beyond is the one really imaginative example of sixteenth-century fantasy gardening in the Boboli—a grotto designed by Bernardo Buontalenti and built between 1583 and 1593. A large artificial cave, it seems to be a huge joke on Man's relation to nature. The walls, once covered in plants that resembled human hair, could at the flick of a concealed tap be covered in a torrent of gushing water, soaking the unprepared visitor and making the half-human, half-animal figures that grow from its walls seem even more bizarrely lifelike than they do now.

In the half light that falls from above you can just make out Poccetti's ceiling paintings of animals set in a jungle of twisted roots and branches. In the corners are Michelangelo's *Slaves* (these are casts, though the originals were here until the beginning of the century) and just visible in the second of the grotto's three chambers is Giambologna's *Venus* wringing out her hair. It is a remarkable monument to the Medicean Grand Dukes at the height of their splendour and at their most stunningly imaginative and thus makes an appropriate place to finish any visit to the Pitti.

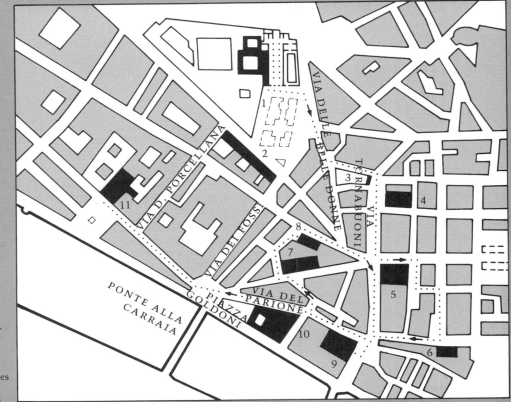

Map 8
S. Maria Novella to Ognissanti

1. S. Maria Novella
2. Loggia di S. Paolo
3. Palazzo Antinori
4. S. Gaetano
5. Palazzo Strozzi
6. Palazzo Davanzati
7. Palazzo Rucellai
8. Rucellai Chapel
9. S. Trinita
10. Palazzo Corsini
11. Ognissanti

N

0   50 100   200 metres

200 yards

S. MARIA NOVELLA
—to—
OGNISSANTI

✤ Until the 1860s the great Dominican basilica of **S. Maria Novella** stood at the threshold of the contado. The land now occupied by the railway station was still a patchwork of gardens and orchards; the roads leading from Piazza S. Maria Novella to the Porta al Prato were bordered by fields where in 1845 John Ruskin, then only 25 years old, would relax after a day of sketching or writing by helping the farmers to bring in their hay. Though such delights are now denied to us, the streets between S. Maria Novella and the Viale being today probably less bucolic and more intensely urban than in any other part of Florence, the Piazza in front of the church still looks much as it did in Ruskin's day. From a café on its east side we can begin the morning by admiring S. Maria Novella's superb façade, which, unlike those of the other large churches in Florence, was completed in the Renaissance.

It was designed by Leon Battista Alberti (1404–72) the extraordinary polymath whose talents as an art theorist, scholar and architect are equally remarkable, and built between 1458 and 1470. As the first attempt to apply a Roman temple front, mathematically calculated to seem balanced and harmonious to the eye, to a traditional Tuscan aisled church, it has an enormous significance in the history of Western ecclesiastical architecture.

At first sight it seems rather a strange combination of different architectural styles, for Alberti was obliged to retain the Gothic arcading along the bottom of the façade and the circular window that lights the nave, both of which were built, along with the rest of the church, in the second half of the thirteenth century. The outstanding achievement of his design is that it manages to accommodate both of these constraints comfortably within a monumental classical organisation that, with its great arched entrance and pedimented upper storey, looks impressively grand and antique.

His most influential innovation was to cover the sloping roofs between the nave and the aisles with the massive scrolls that became the stock in trade of Renaissance and baroque church-façade design in later centuries. Its remarkable elegance is no accident or fluke but based on Alberti's own theories of proportion derived from the study of antique buildings and texts. The upper storey fits exactly twice into the lower storey while the space between them is a third the height of both and the entire façade, if 'rationalised', fits into a square.

The decoration is a strange mixture between the obviously classical—as in the Roman letters beneath the pediment recording the name of Giovanni Rucellai, the church's patron and the head of one of the richest families in early Medicean Florence—and the traditionally Tuscan. It is not difficult to imagine the swirling inlaid patterns on the scrolls or the geometric decoration on the lower-part storey on the façade of S. Miniato or the Baptistery. This decorative jumble, and the formal compromise on which it is based, give S. Maria Novella a curious charm.

The interior is one of the few places south of the Alps where you can recall some of the splendour of the great Gothic cathedrals of northern Europe. As soon as you walk in the door you will see that it is a far more ambitious and elaborate building than the roughly contemporary and similarly sized basilica at the other side of the city—S. Croce, built by the Franciscans. The nave is roofed with a complex vault, and an exaggerated perspective is created by placing each pair of columns slightly closer together as they advance towards the altar. To some extent the differences between the two basilicas express the contrasting attitudes of the religious orders that built them. If S. Croce's simplicity echoes the Franciscan message that there is nothing intimidating about Christian faith, then S. Maria Novella is the product of the more aggressively evangelical Dominicans who took pride in their nickname the 'Hounds of The Lord'.

Unfortunately Giorgio Vasari, court architect and artist to Cosimo I, was given a free hand in the middle of the sixteenth century to efface as much as he could of S. Maria Novella's original Gothic decoration. He removed the rood screen, whitewashed fourteenth-century frescoes and substituted classical for Gothic altars. Much of his work was undone in the early 1860s when the present neo-Gothic altars and windows were installed.

In the place of the second altar on the left nave wall is one of the greatest, if now much restored, paintings of the early Renaissance — the *Trinity* (1), painted (probably in 1425) by the mysterious, short-lived and prodigally gifted Masaccio (1401–1427/8). Above the skeleton at its base is an inscription so macabre that it may well have been suggested by the Dominicans themselves — 'I was that which you are, you will be that which I am.' Its gloomy message is, of course, intended to catch your attention and draw the passer-by into the Christian drama of the painting above. As you look further up, your attention is caught by the Madonna who directs the gaze with a gesture of hand towards the dead body of Christ crucified by the Eternal Father. Though the subject is traditional enough its setting is revolutionary. The wall behind Christ seems to open before our eyes, beneath a magnificent Brunelleschian portal, into a coffered sepulchre constructed according to the then still newly discovered rules of perspective. As in the Brancacci Chapel frescoes the entire scene is flooded with warm golden light that pours over both the architecture and the figures.

The two kneeling figures in the foreground are the patron and his wife, and it may say something significant about the age in which they lived, and the stress the Renaissance laid on the present rather than the hereafter, that through foreshortening they appear to be on the same scale as the Madonna and St John in the painting above.

Map 9
Plan of S. Maria Novella

1. *The Trinity* by Masaccio
2. Strozzi Chapel
3. The Sacristy
4. Gondi Chapel
5. The Chancel
6. Filippo Strozzi Chapel
7. Rucellai Chapel
8. Chiostro Verde
9. Spanish Chapel
10. Chiostrino dei Morti
11. Chiostro Grande
12. Refectory

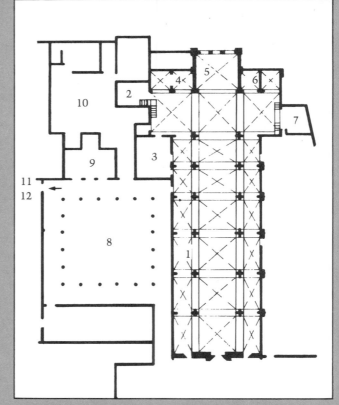

N

0   15   30 metres

100 feet

The Cappella Strozzi (2), occupying the raised presbytery of the original Romanesque church at the top of the steps in the left transept, is a self-contained world where one can feel most easily transported to the Florence of Dante, Petrarch and that slightly later and much more mischievous author, Giovanni Boccaccio (1313–74). Nowhere could we do so more appropriately for S. Maria Novella is the setting for one scene in the introduction to his most successful, scurrilous and famous book, *The Decameron*. The frescoes of Heaven and Hell are probably inspired by the descriptions in Dante's *Divine Comedy*. Painted (by Nardo di Cione) only ten years after the Black Death of 1348 had swept off something like a quarter of the city's population, they illustrate what to us seems no more than a poet's vision but what to a man of the fourteenth century must have seemed a terrifying reality. On the facing wall a stern God surrounded by angels blowing trumpets sends the Blessed to Paradise (on the left wall), and condemns the Damned to the grisly tortures of Hell (to the right). The altarpiece, one of the only examples of a signed and dated panel painting of the mid-fourteenth century, is by Nardo di Cione's richly talented brother, Andrea Orcagna (?–1368), who is more famous as an architect than as a painter. He probably designed both the tabernacle in Or San Michele and the Loggia dei Lanzi. It describes *Christ giving the keys to St Peter and the Book of Knowledge to St Thomas*.

A door at the bottom of the steps leads into the Sacristy (3), a pleasantly opulent room lined with inlaid, gilded furniture. The cupboards down both long walls are early rococo and were made in the 1720s; the more elaborate piece of furniture on the facing wall is late sixteenth-century and was designed by Bernardo Buontalenti. The sacristy makes a strange setting for the painted *Crucifix* above the entrance door attributed to Giotto and thought by some to be his earliest known work (1290–1300) and to be one of the first fully realistic portrayals of the human body in the history of Western painting. It is quite different from any known crucifix of an earlier date. Here Christ's head slumps forward on to His chest, the stomach swells forward below the torso, and the hips grind against the cross.

Few things carried more prestige in Renaissance Florence than a conspicuously located and expensively decorated family chapel and few can have been either more prestigious or more conspicuously located than those along the choir of S. Maria Novella. They were bought, for very large sums, by the richest banking families (though not, surprisingly, by the Medici) and the most sought-after artists were commissioned to paint them. The Cappella Gondi (4) has a fine wooden Crucifix by Brunelleschi and interesting marble decoration by Giuliano da Sangallo. This architect may well have helped Domenico Ghirlandaio to design the colossally grand architectural settings for his masterpiece—*19 Scenes from the Lives of the Virgin, the Baptist and the Dominican Saints* around the chancel (5) commissioned by Giovanni Tornabuoni and painted between 1485 and 1490.

The work of Ghirlandaio, though perhaps less intellectually demanding than that of his contemporaries like Pollaiuolo and Verrocchio, is brilliantly evocative of Florentine high bourgeois life in the late fifteenth century and the most straightforwardly enjoyable art of its period. Vast landscape panoramas sweep into the distance and in the foregrounds the religious narratives are unashamedly used to glorify contemporary life and, of course, the patrons themselves. In a scene from the lower register of the right-hand wall Ludovica Tornabuoni, the patron's daughter, leads a group of women towards St Anne; on the left wall, almost directly opposite, the *Birth of the Virgin* occurs in the Sala Grande of what is probably the Tornabuoni palazzo. Amongst the architectural fantasy he places the occasional tower, street or façade that is recognisably Florentine. The bystanders are mainly portraits of prominent or distinguished men of the day, and it is interesting to observe that the intervening five hundred years has done little to improve the not always beautiful natural features of the typical Florentine male. One of the privileges of the artist was a prominent self-portrait. Ghirlandaio stands to the right in the *Expulsion of St Joachim from the Temple* in the right panel of the lower register of the left wall, wearing a red hat.

Filippo Strozzi, builder of the enormous palace in Via Tornabuoni, bought the chapel to the right of the choir (6) along with a shop in the Mercato Vecchio in 1486. Its frescoes, painted by Filippino Lippi (1456–1504) at the very end of his life are some of the most powerful and strange in late fifteenth- early sixteenth-century Florentine art. Unlike Filippino's rather safe, sub-Botticellian early work they attempt an ambitious fusion of imaginary antique architecture, landscape and figures into a coherent decorative scheme that at first sight looks much later than it in fact is. Painted in a style curiously different from anything contemporary and quite unlike the more decorative work of Ghirlandaio in the choir, they have a strange energetic restlessness and violence that anticipates Florentine Mannerist painting of the next generation.

To the right St Philip tames a Dragon on the steps of the temple of Mars, before summoning from it a stench so vile that it kills the heathen king to the right. In the lunette above, different heathens (here writhing, gesticulating and musculated caricatures) are showing St Philip no mercy, at the age of 87, as they put him to a painful martyr's death. In the opposite lunette St John the Evangelist is being boiled in oil on the orders of the Roman Emperor Domitian, and in the larger panel below he raises Drusiana from the dead. The tomb on the end wall is by Benedetto da Maiano (1442–97).

The Cappella Rucellai (7) at the end of the right transept was raised to its present height in the fifteenth century to balance with the Cappella Strozzi in the opposite transept. It used to contain the wonderful Rucellai Madonna by Duccio that Nathaniel Hawthorne, writing in 1858, wished could be '. . . borne out of the church in another triumphal procession (like the one which brought it there) and reverently burnt', which is a reminder of for how very long even sensitive and well-informed critics despised the 'primitives'. It was eventually born out of the church, to be reverently hung in the Uffizi. The most interesting work of art now to be seen is a beautiful tomb slab by Ghiberti, though the real purpose of walking up the steps into the chapel is to enjoy the view across the church before walking back to the other end of the nave and walking out of the entrance.

Immediately to the left of the church (if we are

looking at the façade from the Piazza) is the Chiostro Verde (8), so called because of the greenish frescoes by Paolo Uccello of *Scenes from the Old Testament* that once covered most of its walls (opening times, see p. 231). Most of these have deteriorated badly but one remarkable lunette, thought to be his masterpiece, *The Flood*, survives adequately well to give some idea of Uccello's truly amazing abilities as a painter. It represents, occasionally with revolting realism, the horrors of a religious cataclysm—in this case the flood survived by Noah and the occupants of the ark. Two arks, one (to the left) afloat and the other on dry land, converge to give the idea of a deeply receding space. Their foreground, and the space between them, is occupied by an assortment of fighting, decaying, drowning and starving people, all painted with the scientific accuracy with which Uccello was clearly obsessed. The two fighting horsemen in the left foreground are even made to wear black and white bangles around their necks to provide Uccello with a perspectival challenge worthy of his genius.

At the other side of the cloister is the Spanish Chapel (9) painted between 1346 and 1357 by Andrea da Firenze, a Florentine artist about whom almost nothing is known. Ruskin called the highly decorative, monumental frescoes 'the most noble piece of pictorial philosophy in Italy'. The key to the paintings is on the ceiling: each of its vaulted quarters relates to the wall frescoes below. Taken as a whole the frescoes represent the Dominican ideal of the Christian way of life. On the left wall is the Contemplative Life and its necessary attainments as expounded by St Thomas Aquinas—learning and religious knowledge. The scenes on the right represent the Active Life, with the church militant symbolised by the Duomo, here in a projected form as the actual building was not roofed until the 1430s. The Inquisition sat in the Spanish Chapel during the late sixteenth and seventeenth centuries, no doubt because they found its ambience invigoratingly austere.

The Chiostro Verde leads to the Chiostrino dei Morti (10), the oldest part of S. Maria Novella and worth a quick visit. On the west side, again of the Chiostro Verde, there is a view into the Chiostro

Grande (11) where you see, sadly, not learned-looking monks but those equally vigilant and admirable contemporary guardians of Italian morality, the Carabinieri, who seem to spend a large part of their day jogging around its perimeter walls, an activity which is probably less boring than it sounds as they are frescoed by Bronzino, Poccetti and other great artists. In the Refectory (12) there is a rather dull collection of reliquaries and some fine paintings by Alessandro Allori, the most important painter in Florence during the second half of the sixteenth century.

* * *

So much for the church and the cloisters. Now we emerge into the Piazza. (37) The two marble obelisks sitting on pretty bronze tortoises were placed here by Cosimo I as markers at either end of the course for a new chariot race which, until it was discontinued in the last century, was considered the Florentine answer to the Palio in Siena. At the far end of the Piazza is an elegant late fifteenth-century building, the Loggia di S. Paolo, that owes much to the Ospedale degli Innocenti by Brunelleschi in the Piazza SS. Annunziata. From the left of the Piazza (if we have our backs to the church) leads the Via delle Belle Donne, probably so called for the quality of its late medieval brothels. If you follow it and take the first left up Via del Trebbio you arrive in the small Piazza Antinori at the top of Via Tornabuoni and find yourself standing between two of the most beautiful buildings in Florence.

The façade of **Palazzo Antinori**, composed of identically sized and smooth blocks of golden stone (mid-fifteenth century, architect unknown) looks superb from close to though it is really intended as an elegant termination to the Via Tornabuoni and to be seen from a distance. The same stone was used in the 1640s to build the magnificent high baroque façade of **S. Gaetano** roughly opposite. This was designed by Gherardo Silvani (1579–1675) who sets off the fine colour and texture of the stone with a generous sprinkling of white marble flourishes. Though impressive, it is perhaps not quite comparable to the finest churches in Rome of the same period by Bernini, Borromini or Cortona.

Unfortunately it is seldom open, though this is

37

not quite the disappointment that it might be, as the money ran out before Silvani could create a correspondingly lavish interior. To its right is a café selling the most delicious *crostini*.

A little further down Via Tornabuoni, on the left, is the last, the largest and the grandest of the great Renaissance palazzi. It was built over a period of about forty years, from 1489 to the mid-1530s, by the Strozzi, a family whose wealth and importance in Renaissance Florence was second only to that of the Medici. One of the best places to get an idea both of the technical excellence of its construction and of its rather appealing enormity is from a café in Piazza degli Strozzi, which faces the entrance façade, to reach which you must turn left at the traffic lights, and then first right.

The design, which is variously attributed to Giuliano da Sangallo and Benedetto da Maiano, is highly conservative even by the standards of Florentine domestic architecture. Perhaps on the insistence of the patron, Filippo Strozzi, it deliberately turns its back on innovation and instead makes all the traditional elements of the Florentine palazzo bigger and more imposing than

ever before. A businessman of genius who amassed one of the great fortunes of the late fifteenth-century Europe through banking, Filippo Strozzi was a less enlightened patron of the arts than his contemporary and rival Lorenzo de' Medici. The construction of his palazzo called for the remodelling of this entire vicinity, as its rectangular plan simply bulldozed its way through the surrounding honeycomb of shops and lanes.

Looking at the photograph overleaf, taken in the last century before the destruction of the Mercato Vecchio, we can imagine how overpoweringly impressive the **Palazzo Strozzi (38)** must originally have seemed as it rose from the tangle of streets around it. Even today, when these have been replaced by new buildings of a completely different size and scale, it makes a great impact. The external walls alone cover something rather more than an acre; the cornice, copied from antique buildings in Rome, projects six feet from the façade. 'Imagine demolishing the Palazzo Strozzi in Florence,' said Aldous Huxley; 'it would be about as easy to demolish the Matterhorn.' Yet despite its solidity it is not a particularly clumsy building. The stone blocks, cut in repeating patterns, are decorative in themselves, while the façade through its simplicity achieves the classical clarity and grandeur intended by its builder.

The fourteenth-century **Palazzo Davanzati**, nearby in Via Porta Rossa (turn left into Via D. Anselmi, then right into Piazza Davanzati), is a very different building. Its façade, if you remove the top-floor loggia and the family crest, which are sixteenth-century additions, is one of the few surviving buildings in Florence in which you can perceive the transition from a late-medieval fortress tower to the Renaissance palazzo. The interior, now the **Museo della Casa Antica Fiorentina** (opening times, see p. 229) is one of the most delightful museums I know. Though its rooms are largely reconstructions following a disastrous division into flats in the middle of the last century, and though the pictures and furniture are really from houses and museums all over the city, it nevertheless gives a convincing impression to the visitor that he is entering the world of early Renaissance Florence. It provides a window on to the domestic life of one, admittedly highly excep-

38

tional, family of Florentine merchants no less than Iris Origo's classic portrait of Francesco Datini, *The Merchant of Prato*, a reading of which is the best possible preparation for a visit.

The loggia, which you enter from the street, would probably always have been rented out as a shop or a small factory. It is only when you walk through the small, heavily bolted door at its far side that we enter the heart of the palazzo. This leads into the courtyard, an immensely evocative and atmospheric space where one can almost hear and smell the endless activities and commotions — the shouts of the mistress scolding her servants or the clatter of feet on the stairs — that must have made up the daily life of a large household.

By the standards of the age, when even a very rich and successful man would expect to live, with his family, servants and animals, in no more than five or six rooms, the Palazzo Davanzati is amazingly large. To have a private courtyard, with its own well, in the centre of a city where space was a vastly expensive luxury and privacy a privilege undreamt of except by the richest of the rich, must

have seemed astounding to a Florentine of the day. It is possible to reconstruct with some accuracy how and for what the early occupants used most of the rooms in their palazzo. The two small ones at the far side of the courtyard were storerooms for provisions. Caution was not simply the watchword of the typical fourteenth-century merchant — it was his obsession. Even the most casually optimistic or happy-go-lucky family would take care to keep at least a year's supply of grain, oil and other essentials in stock in order to survive either a famine or a siege.

Though grand, impressive, and, if we look at the staircase as it leaps up five stories on climbing arches and *sporti* projecting from the walls, rather beautiful, it is hard to avoid the conclusion that the Palazzo Davanzati would not have been a particularly comfortable or convenient place to live. The storerooms on the ground floor are separated from the kitchens (which as in all Florentine palazzi until the seventeenth century are on the top floor) by more than 150 steps, though there is a lift to wind things up and down. Originally the courtyard would have been open to the elements and for much of the year rather cold. However, all sympathy for the early Davanzati (or Davizi, as the original builders were confusingly called) soon disappears when you climb the stairs (passing a faded *St Christopher* on the landing) to the first floor and turn into the Sala Grande, a truly magnificent room equipped with all the comforts that the fourteenth century could offer. There are glass panes in the windows, brick tiles on the floor, two stone fireplaces with flues built into the walls to carry away the smoke, and even a painted ceiling. Both this and the even richer room next door, the Sala dei Papagalli (which was probably a dining room) would have been used only for a few days a year, if there was a family wedding, or for an important religious feast. The most beautiful room in the house is the bedroom on the next floor, equipped with the most up-to-date conveniences, like a connecting lavatory. The walls are entirely covered in bright, patterned frescoes intended (in a not uncharacteristic attempt to save money) as a substitute for vastly expensive tapestry, and creating a warm, almost cosy atmosphere. They are so cleverly painted that one really imagines that they are hanging, as the artist pretends, from silken ropes and that above them runs a loggia full of exotic birds and flowers.

The pieces of furniture in this room are some of the finest surviving examples of their period. Though not the world's most comfortable chairs, beds and stools, they are beautifully made and decorated. The enormous double bed with a platform around it and a carved, inlaid head was an essential status symbol for any well-off family. In the rectangular trunks, known as *cassoni*, which were usually given as wedding presents and decorated, as here, with a prettily painted front panel, the mistress of the house would probably have kept the family linen.

When not looking after or counting her linen she could probably have been found upstairs in the kitchens supervising her staff as they cooked the heavy and heavily spiced food that was the preferred diet of her husband and family. Just how large that staff was is not easy to say with any accuracy, but as there are no servants' bedrooms it can safely be assumed that they all slept on the floor, probably of the kitchen as it would have been the warmest room in the house. It would also, until the end of the fifteenth century, have certainly included several slaves, usually female, who were bought (preferably before they were ten years old) in the markets of Genoa and Venice. They had no rights of any kind whatever. Their owners could 'have, hold, sell, alienate, exchange, enjoy, rent or unrent, dispose of in his will, judge soul and body and do with in perpetuity whatsoever may please him' with them. The rights of the master of the house over his wife and children were almost as great. His wife was expected to leave the house only to go to church. His daughter would be taught to read and write only if she wished to be a nun and, if not, would be married to the partner of her father's choice soon after she reached the marriageable age of twelve—the men of the Renaissance attached little significance to the concept of female emancipation.

With Palazzo Davanzati and Palazzo Strozzi in mind, let us consider another fine example of Florentine domestic architecture—**Palazzo Rucellai**. If you turn left out of Palazzo Davanzati and walk back to Via Tornabuoni (passing on the left the very pretty Palazzo Bartolini-Salimbeni, see page 124), cross to Via del Parione, taking the first right and then the first left into Via del Purgatorio, you will approach its principal façade from the best possible angle. It was built about a century later than Palazzo Davanzati and is probably the most important example of domestic architecture in Florence. Running flush with the north side of Via Vigna Nuova and forming one side of the small triangular Piazza Rucellai, the façade is a sophisticated composition of differently sized rusticated stone blocks divided into rhythmical, proportioned bays by pilasters and architraves. Although, ironically, it had little influence in Florence, Alberti's strictly theoretical application of the classical orders as decoration became the basis of the high Renaissance architectural style of Bramante, Raphael and Michelangelo.

If the most fascinating fifteenth-century Florentine palazzo, it is also one of the worst documented. Although generally accepted on stylistic grounds as the design of Alberti and to have been built between the late 1440s and early 1450s, there is nothing to prove the case and some plausible arguments to the contrary. Unfortunately the patron, the same Giovanni Rucellai responsible for the façade of S. Maria Novella, in an autobiography that seems almost deliberately designed to frustrate and torment architectural historians, never mentions the dates of construction or the name of the architect. Those who argue against an attribution to Alberti point to the Medici device of intersecting rings on the first floor entablature which can only date from post 1461 when, after Giovanni's greatest coup in the game of Florentine marital politics, his son became engaged to the daughter of Piero de' Medici. This could only mean that it was built after the very similar Palazzo Piccolomini in Pienza by Bernardo Rosellino. Those who argue in favour of Alberti, on the other hand, point out his previous involvement with the Rucellai over other projects and argue that he was the only personality of the mid-fifteenth century capable of so original and unusual a design that displays a thorough knowledge of classical architectural theory. The loggia to the right of the Piazza, though messily finished, was probably also designed by Alberti and built specifically for the Medici/Rucellai wedding celebrations.

It is worth walking around behind Palazzo Rucellai in order to see the Rucellai Chapel in San Pancrazio. (Its opening times are eccentric; we must hope that we are in luck.) It is now entered from No. 18 Via della Spada which is best reached by walking around the back of Palazzo Rucellai (passing the Trattoria Latini) and up Via de' Federighi. It was designed by Alberti in 1467 to house Giovanni Rucellai's funerary monument, which is an imaginary recreation in miniature of the Sanctuary of the Holy Sepulchre in Jerusalem. Judged by the canons of classical architecture this is generally considered to be the purest of Alberti's buildings. The aedicule sits like an enormous jewel among plain grey walls sparsely enriched by stone decoration and beneath what is probably the first barrel vault in Renaissance architecture. The effect is convincingly antique.

If you walk back along Via della Spada to Via Tornabuoni and turn right you will reach the church of **S. Trinita**. The façade, by Bernardo

Buontalenti, is an interesting if hesitant combination of Renaissance and something approaching the baroque. The interior is very different. A sombre grey light falls around a double row of columns supporting a rib-vaulted ceiling. The odd candle glimmers in a side-chapel, throwing a weak light against the gold background to an altarpiece. To step into the nave is to enter the deeply pious world of fourteenth-century Tuscany, when most of the church was built.

The Bartolini-Salimbeni Chapel (4th chapel, right nave) is one of the very few of its date that cretains, in almost unaltered form, its original decoration. It is enclosed by a fifteenth-century wrought-iron grille; the altarpiece and the wall frescoes have remained as and where they were in the 1420s when painted by Lorenzo Monaco (1370–c.1425), a Sienese artist who lived and painted mainly in Florence. His work, like that of other artists of the International Gothic style, combines highly refined, delicate and realistic detail in bright colours with a quality of fantasy. In the main panel of the altarpiece of the *Annunciation* the angel Gabriel spreads his wings to reveal rose, violet, pink and blue feathers while the Madonna, half lost in the book on her lap, sits among robes that fall to the ground in a series of graceful, flowing lines. It is from Lorenzo Monaco, and in particular from this altarpiece that Fra Angelico seems to have evolved his early style.

The Sassetti Chapel, in the right transept (second to the right of the chancel) was frescoed by Domenico Ghirlandaio between 1482 and 1485, immediately before he began the even more lively and ambitious frescoes around the chancel of S. Maria Novella. Their nominal subject is *Scenes from the Life of St Francis* but one walks away from it thinking not so much about the saint and his life as of the patron, Francesco Sassetti (whose portrait is to the right of the altar), his family and his friends, whose magnificent way of life they evoke and whose taste for realistic portraiture and impeccable craftsmanship they undoubtedly reflect. Ghirlandaio leaves the spectator in no doubt as to the importance and wealth of Francesco Sassetti. He is dressed with all the understated opulence favoured by the grandest high bourgeois merchants of his age. A rich crimson gown trimmed with fur is held together by a wide black girdle to which is attached a purse bulging with florins, the Florentine golden coin whose name was to be adopted all over Europe. The ships, towers, distant mountain ranges and a church with a spire in the background allude to his frequent travels abroad.

Interestingly, Ghirlandaio gives the great religious events in his fresco such as *St Francis Being Conferred the Right to Rule* (upper register, facing wall) recognisably Florentine background scenery. In the foreground St Francis is meeting the Pope; behind is the Piazza della Signoria (note—still without the Piazza degli Uffizi). The scene below is set in the Piazza S. Trinita before Cosimo erected the marble column at its centre and Buontalenti added the existing façade to this church. The altarpiece (1485) of the *Adoration of the Shepherds* is one of Ghirlandaio's most beautiful paintings and shows an obvious debt in its technique and imagery to the Portinari altarpiece by Hugo van der Goes (now in the Uffizi), possibly the first northern European painting to arrive in Florence.

In the second chapel of the left transept is Luca della Robbia's tomb of Bishop Benozzo Federighi, considered one of his most touching works. The dead Christ in the central panel and the face of the Bishop are particularly fine. In the fifth chapel of the left nave there is a *Penitent Magdalene* by Desiderio da Settignano and Benedetto da Maiano, both important younger contemporaries of Donatello, a work which may have inspired that artist's own Magdalene in the Museo dell' Opera del Duomo. The first chapel has a very dark but clearly rather beautiful ceiling by Poccetti. On the entrance wall you can see the remains of the earlier Romanesque church effaced in a series of unbelievably complicated rebuildings in the fourteenth and fifteenth centuries.

The side door from S. Trinita takes us back into Via del Parione. If here we turn left we shall pass along the back of Palazzo Corsini (the gallery can be visited by appointment, see page 221) and then of the less imposing Palazzo Ricasoli before reaching Piazza Goldoni, named after, and with a statue of, Italy's most famous comic dramatist of the eighteenth century, Carlo Goldoni, who is, we may note, a Venetian (comic drama not being the Florentine forte). But Piazza Goldoni is a noisy place to linger so we shall continue down the Borgo Ognissanti past a good example of Art Nouveau on the right and the Ospedale di S. Giovanni with a fine baroque double staircase (No. 20) to **Ognissanti**, a church founded by breakaway Franciscans in the late thirteenth century. Looking at the façade (1637, by Matteo Nigetti), a rather flat example of early baroque, or the dull, mainly late eighteenth-century, interior, you may be disappointed. But there is an appealing ceiling fresco of *St Francis in Glory* by N. Romei (1770) and if you walk up the nave, turn into the left transept and leave the church by the facing door you will find yourself in a delightful cloister, into which, on the entrance side, a part of the original fourteenth-century church charmingly protrudes. A door on the right side leads to the refectory. On the far wall is another great fresco by Domenico Ghirlandaio, the *Last Supper*, in which he skilfully creates an atmosphere of intense calm and civilisation. Christ and the Apostles eat among orange and lemon trees. Above them a peacock hops on to a window ledge and other birds fly through the air. The calm and civilisation contrasts with the excited faces of the Apostles who, with the exception of Judas (third to the right of Christ), all disclaim the betrayal. To either side of the Last Supper are two portrayals of saints as scholars surrounded by books. On the left is Ghirlandaio's *St Jerome* (1480). *St Augustine* to the right is an early work by Botticelli (1480).

Near Ognissanti there are some good restaurants. Just around the corner is the crowded, cheap and very good Sostanza at Via del Porcellana 25r. If we return to the Piazza S. Trinita there is Natale or for something simpler and cheaper you need only cross the Ponte alla Carraia from Piazza Goldoni to Angiolino at Via S. Spirito 36r (second left).

Map 10
SS. Annunziata, the
Accademia and S. Ambrogio

1. Ospedale degli Innocenti
2. SS. Annunziata
3. Accademia
4. Opificio delle Pietre Dure
5. S. Maria Maddalena dei Pazzi
6. Casa Buonarroti
7. S. Ambrogio

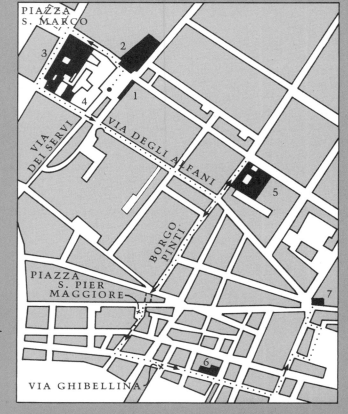

N

0   100   200 metres

200 yards

9

SS. ANNUNZIATA, THE ACCADEMIA
—*and*—
S. MARIA MADDALENA DEI PAZZI

✤ The best coffee in Florence, according to those who claim to know, is to be found at Robiglio's in Via dei Servi (No. 112). Whether or not this is true, it is a good place to begin any walk since looking either way from its entrance you see Florence at its grandest. To the south, Brunelleschi's cupola and the Duomo are seen at their most impressive—a cliff of green and white marble sheared and scarred by a pattern of buttresses, walls and windows, by patches of dark shadow and splashes of livid colour, rises from the end of the street, creating a contrast in scale that is always breathtaking, no matter how often it is seen. To the north, a bronze Grand Duke stands at the centre of the arcaded Piazza SS. Annunziata and stares down a monumental axis worthy of baroque Rome.

Walking towards Robiglio's from the Duomo is delightful. We can hardly take a step without having to stop and admire some sight or another. At the entrance to Via dei Pucci is the Palazzo Pucci which, occupying an entire block, is one of the largest if not one of the lightest in Florence and the home of the Marchese Emilio Pucci, the flamboyant couturier who still lives in some of its 500 rooms. The central part of the façade is sixteenth-century and attributed to Ammanati. On the opposite side of the street is the little church of S. Michele Visdomini with an undistinguished interior but an early Pontormo of the *Holy Family and Saints* (1518) in the right aisle. A little further on is the fine Palazzo Niccolini (No. 15, on the left, 1548–50), which combines the more endearing qualities of mid-sixteenth-century palazzi. Equally fine and of roughly the same date is the brick Palazzo Grifoni, to the left at the entrance to the Piazza. At Robligio's (on the right) you stop for that coffee before continuing into the Piazza, from the near corner of which you enjoy almost the same view as in the engraving by Zocchi. (**39**) If no longer the restful place that it was in the eighteenth century, the Piazza has an air of civilisation that seems especially agreeable in a city of intimidating stone palazzi and tall claustrophobic streets. Its unity tends to mislead the visitor into thinking that it was all designed and built at the same time when in fact this is far from the case. Brunelleschi's famous **Ospedale degli Innocenti** (to the right as we face the church) was begun in 1421 and is the first building to apply fully classical ornament and a system of proportion to the Tuscan Romanesque tradition. Only the nine central bays are by Brunelleschi, those to either side being added in the sixteenth century. It is thought to be the first foundling hospital in the world and, remarkably, it still remains as one today. It suffered a chequered early history: after prospering for its first fifty years, the orphanage seems to have run into financial difficulties, as in the early 1480s several of the children lodged there died from malnutrition. It was after this disaster that Andrea della Robbia was commissioned to make the ten medallions (the two at either end are nineteenth-century imitations) of swaddled babies that seem so sweetly to appeal for sympathy and charity. In his novel *A Room with a View* E. M. Forster mocked their sentimentality. Lucy Honeychurch, his naive heroine, after spending a miserable half-hour accompanied and misdirected by the gushing Miss Lavish, finds herself standing in the 'square of the Annunziata and saw in the living terracotta those divine babies whom no cheap imitation can ever stale. There they stood, with their shining limbs bursting from the garments of charity, and their strong white arms extended against circlets of heaven. Lucy thought she had never seen anything more beautiful . . .'

39

Walking into the first courtyard and up to the first floor, we come to the Innocenti Gallery, which contains some good examples of fifteenth-century sculpture and painting including the *Adoration of the Magi* (1488) by Domenico Ghirlandaio and a fine altarpiece by Piero di Cosimo.

The Loggia of the Servites at the other side of the Piazza is a hundred years later. It was built in imitation of the Ospedale degli Innocenti between 1516 and 1525. In the first decade of the seventeenth century the Pucci family paid for (we are left in no doubt of this by the inscription on the entablature) the portico on the Annunziata, completing the Piazza.

Rising from a sea of shiny Fiats is the equestrian statue of Ferdinand I, the most dedicated and talented of Cosimo's heirs. It was begun by Giambologna after much coaxing in 1607 (a year before his death when he was already 78 years old) and finished by his pupil Pietro Tacca. Though there are minor differences in detail, it is very largely a copy of his equally magnificent statue of Cosimo I in the Piazza della Signoria, though Ferdinand rather benefits from his superior position. He sym-bolises the Counter-Reformation Prince and the monument is appropriately cast from the bronze of Ottoman guns captured at the battle of Lepanto, when the combined Catholic powers thought they had driven the Turks from the western Mediterranean. If inclined towards the slightly tedious pomposity characteristic of the later Medici, Ferdinand (Grand Duke from 1587 to 1609) was an efficient and enlightened ruler. He can claim the dubious honour of being the founder of Leghorn, the now very unattractive port just south of Pisa, which he declared a free city open to those of any religion. Within a century it had grown from an oversized village to become the second largest city in Tuscany.

The pair of fountains that flank Ferdinand are also by Pietro Tacca and are perhaps the most interesting and bizarre examples of Florentine baroque art—if also the most grotesque. In bright, poisonous green, their surface is a writhing mass of repellent sea creatures, a mélange of tails and tendrils, of gills, lips, eyes and soft rippling bumps. But if not everyone's idea of beauty, they are a rare fusion of imagination and technical skill.

From the portico on the northern side of the Piazza we enter the fifteenth-century Chiostro dei Voti which was once filled with 600 different wax effigies of pilgrims who had visited **SS. Annunziata**. Thankfully these have now been burnt, lost or thrown away, allowing the visitor to concentrate on the superb frescoes around the walls. The majority of the scenes are by Andrea del Sarto (1486–1531), an artist much admired by Michelangelo and still considered the supreme painter of the Florentine high Renaissance style though he is not today quite as fashionable as he once was. This is perhaps because Bernard Berenson, that mighty influence on twentieth-century taste, once dismissed his paintings as being '. . . like beautiful deaf and dumb children; at their best you expect them to speak. They never do.'

The earliest scene, however, is the *Nativity* on the facing wall to the left of the door. This dates from 1460 and is by Alessio Baldovinetti. Though badly deteriorated, the landscape, spreading over a vast plain with mountains in the distance, is still recognisably lovely. Andrea del Sarto is responsible for the five scenes on the left wall. These were painted in 1509–10 and Sarto scholars excuse their strange stiffness by claiming that this was probably the artist's first experience of painting in fresco. Much, much more impressive is his *Birth of the Virgin* of five years later (the furthest scene to the left of the right wall, to the left of the relief of the *Madonna* by Michelozzo). But just as fine are two different scenes by his two young pupils Rosso Fiorentino (1495–1540) and Jacopo Pontormo (1494–1556) then at the outset of their careers but destined to become the outstanding artists of the next decade and the leading early Mannerists. These paintings are their first important works. In Pontormo's *Visitation* (the scene furthest to the left when facing the entrance wall) his style is still so closely modelled on his master's that it has often been mistaken for the work of Sarto. Rosso strays further from Sarto's influence in his tortured and unclassical *Assumption* of 1517 (to the right of Pontormo's *Visitation*).

The right panel of the right wall represents the *Marriage of the Virgin* (1514) by Franciabigio, a mysterious and clearly highly neurotic artist who vented his rage against the monks of SS.

Annunziata, whom he thought had insulted him in exhibiting the painting before completion, by destroying the face of the Madonna. It was later repainted by another hand but this has now been removed leaving the patch of bare plaster that he intended.

SS. Annunziata has probably the grandest and certainly the most fully baroque interior of any Florentine church. Walking into the nave for the first time the visitor experiences a wonderful sensation of surprise and excitement. The blinding magnificence of sparkling gilt and marble bathed in yellowish light, while it might not be entirely unexpected in Naples or Rome, is so different from the interior of any other Florentine church and so sharply in contrast to the severity of the Piazza outside that, for a moment at least, it stuns the senses. SS. Annunziata is the only church in Florence where one can experience the full, self-confident blast of the Counter-Reformation and the opulent grandeur of the Catholic Church in the sixteenth and seventeenth centuries. It looks its best when bursting with people on a Sunday or at Easter, and a choral Mass by Palestrina booms from the organ accompanied by the floating voices of basses, trebles and tenors, or alternatively in the evening when lit by hundreds of flickering, spluttering and pungent candles.

Founded in 1250, SS. Annunziata grew more famous and richer than other Florentine churches owing to the fame of the *Miraculous Image of the Virgin Annunciate* now in the tempietto to the left of the entrance. By the fifteenth century this was attracting so many pilgrims, who came from all over Europe in search of miracles, that in 1444 the Medici commissioned Michelozzo to pull down the original foundation and build a new and larger church.

His design combines the conventional with the unusual. The nave is wide and open in the traditional way, with chapels to either side, but at the far end of the church is a polygonal tribune based on the surviving temple of Minerva in Rome. Alberti is thought to have designed the triumphal arch linking the tribune to the nave. The austerity of the fifteenth-century church combines successfully with the rich baroque interior. This is largely the work of G. Foggini, though the fabulous gilded ceiling and the *Assumption* at its centre is by Volterrano (1611–89), a leading Tuscan baroque painter.

As so often in very grand baroque churches, the general effect is much more impressive than the works of art and chapels when taken individually. But the tempietto with a fifteenth-century marble core by Michelozzo, later enriched with a baroque canopy, is very fine. It was paid for by the Medici to house the *Miraculous Image of the Virgin*, which is usually hidden behind a cloth on the back wall; on the floor an inscription (very difficult to see) applauds their munificence without any false modesty—'The marble alone cost 4,000 florins.' Then the Feroni chapel (the first to the left), built between 1690 and 1693 and like all good baroque decoration in Florence the work of G. Foggini, is most impressive. It owes a good deal to the work of Bernini though Foggini achieves the same spiralling, soaring effects without open imitation.

The painting above the altar, the subject of which is the *Vision of St Julian* (c. 1455), is no less interesting than the architecture, since it is by Andrea del Castagno—perhaps the most gifted of the artists in the generation that followed Masaccio. His paintings have a highly charged, usually violent emotion created by realistic figure-drawing and sharp contrasts in colour. Like Masaccio his painting is heavily influenced by contemporary sculpture, and in particular by the work of Donatello. On the basis of an entirely fictional story in Vasari's *Lives of the Artists* that Castagno murdered his contemporary Domenico Veneziano, the Church officially 'blacked' his art from the end of the sixteenth century. This fresco was only rediscovered in 1864. A detached fresco representing *St Jerome Praying to the Trinity*, also by Castagno, has been hung above the altar in the next chapel on this side of the nave, where it looks a little uncomfortable amid late sixteenth-century paintings by Alessandro Allori (1535–1607) that imitate the late style of Michelangelo.

On the opposite side of the nave, in the fifth chapel from the entrance to the church, is Bernardo Rossellino's tomb of Orlando de' Medici, an obscure cousin of Cosimo il Vecchio of whom we cannot be expected to have heard. The fine *Pietà* to the right of the entrance to the tribuna is by Baccio Bandinelli, the almost universally detested sculptor who was Cellini's mortal enemy. It has a faintly macabre history attached to it, since it was made for his father's tomb, but a premature death from the plague ensured that it became his own. The tribuna, usually entered through a corridor near the Sacristy (follow the signs to 'confessions'), has eight chapels of which three are of interest. In the first after the confessional there is a fifteenth-century *Madonna and Saints* in the manner of Perugino. In the next is Bronzino's great *Resurrection* which, behind its superficial polish, betrays signs of his later more complicated and agitated Counter-Reformation style and serves to remind us that Bronzino is important not only for his portraits. On the central axis of the church is the chapel decorated by Giambologna which contains his own tomb. The solemn and dark early seventeenth-century paintings (the *Resurrection* to the right is by Passignano, and the *Lamentation* on the rear wall is by Ligozzi) and the frescoes by Poccetti all strike an appropriately sombre note.

A door from the left transept leads to the tranquil Chiostro dei Morti. In the lunette above the entrance is one of Andrea del Sarto's most famous paintings—*The Madonna del Sacco* (1525). On the entrance side of the cloisters is the Cappella di S. Luca containing the graves of several artists including Cellini and Pontormo and some fine paintings including Pontormo's early *Holy Family* (1514). If the sacristan is to be found, ask him to open the chapel.

* * *

If on returning to the Piazza you turn right down Via Cesare Battisti to the Piazza S. Marco, then walk a short way down Via Ricasoli, you arrive at the **Galleria dell' Academia**, which contains the single most famous piece of Renaissance sculpture, without a visit to which, I suppose, no visit to Florence can seem complete—the *David* by Michelangelo. It was removed from the Piazza della Signoria in 1873, where it was felt that the otherwise lovable pigeons were doing it less than no good, and placed in a circular tribune especially designed by Emilio de' Fabbris (who was later to design the façade of the Duomo) in the Galleria dell' Accademia. If you walk into the Piazza S.

Marco and then turn left, past the Florentine Art School and into Via Ricasoli (at No. 66 is the University School of Architecture where at the time of writing (1985) there are 6,096 potential Brunelleschis enrolled as students), you arrive at the gallery entrance.

At either side of the entrance to Room I hang a pair of paintings of saints by Fra Bartolomeo, a key Florentine high Renaissance artist roughly contemporary with Andrea del Sarto. These are worth more than an admiring glance before entering the Salone di Michelangelo. In the tribune at the far end stands the *David*. As with other endlessly reproduced works of art, like the *Mona Lisa* or the *Birth of Venus*, the *David* is well known, to say the least, to everyone who visits the gallery. There is something, however, that generally surprises visitors encountering the original—its immense size. Standing at over 16 feet, it was by far the largest free-standing figure to have been made by any European artist since antiquity. It was certainly its size that most impressed Michelangelo's contemporaries who regarded the sheer technical achievement of carving so large a figure from a single block of marble as almost superhuman. It seems all the more staggering since the block from which it was carved, rather too thin for its height and already damaged by different sculptors who had tried to make something of it during the course of the fifteenth century, imposed severe limitations on his freedom of design.

Visitors to Florence since the sixteenth century have all seen the *David* but for some reason few of them have said anything very amusing about it. D. H. Lawrence described the David on different occasions as 'the Genius of Florence' and as 'the incarnation of the modern self-conscious young man, and very objectionable'. Hawthorne thought the stance stiff and compared it to that of an actor in a provincial playhouse. Most, however, have simply been awed into silence. A little more on its history: Michelangelo began the *David* when he was 26, in 1501. It was finished before he was thirty, in 1504, and immediately established his reputation. Its success was so great that for the rest of his life he worked only for the grandest patrons of the age. Originally intended for the

Cathedral, it was placed instead outside the Palazzo della Signoria, and it is not difficult to see why—the subject is richly symbolic of the triumph of the new Florentine Republic which had expelled the Medici in 1494, though whether it was Michelangelo's intention to invest the *David* with any political significance whatsoever is not certain.

From the *David* we turn to the *Slaves*, intended for the tomb of Pope Julius II which, had it been completed, would have been Michelangelo's masterpiece and one of the great artistic achievements of the high Renaissance. Opinions on the *Slaves'* artistic value differ greatly. On the one hand it is argued that they remain incompleteonly because Michelangelo was never permitted to finish them by his demanding and impatient patrons, that they are largely the work of assistants, barely blocked out and as artistically unimportant to his intended final product as are the foundations to a building. The other point of view is that they are some of his greatest work, throwing a beam of light into the immense complications of Michelangelo's creative personality and

the clearest physical representation of his concept of the sculpture as the prisoner of the block and the soul as the captive of the body.

Though in different states of completion, all four of the *Slaves*, which date from between 1519 and 1536, are well enough defined to describe not only violent physical actions but also the extremes of human emotion. Looking at them carefully it is possible to see the contrasts between the work of Michelangelo and the rough 'blocking out' of his assistants. On the shoulder of the *Awakening Slave* (first to the right), the crude punches of a heavy chisel suddenly turn into a delicate fretted web of tiny lines working in a pattern that turns the material into a living, breathing, swelling surface. Michelangelo's hand is no less obvious on the *Bearded Slave* (second right), *Atlas* with his head half concealed in stone and the *Young Slave* with his head half covered by an arm. It is easy, looking at finished sculpture, to forget the immense physical labour of carving in marble. To produce a finished work like the *David* or the *Pietà* in St Peter's is a Herculean task that begins with modelling in wax or clay and only ends with the use of abrasives which, when rubbed repeatedly over the carved surface, produce a smooth texture.

The more finished *St Matthew* (1505–8, the central figure to the right) is the first and last of a dozen figures that Michelangelo optimistically agreed to carve for the Florentine Cathedral authorities before success swept him to Rome and the greater commissions offered by the Papacy.

The Palestrina *Pietà* (to the right before the *David*) is not now generally attributed to Michelangelo. It was discovered during the last century in S. Maria di Palestrina, a church outside Rome, from which it was purchased and given to Florence by an anonymous donor in 1940. Those who doubt the attribution argue that the torso is anatomically incorrect (though this is also true of some Michelangelo drawings) and that the *Pietà*'s composition is an inverted form of Michelangelo's *Pietà* now in the Museo dell' Opera del Duomo. Whatever the outcome of these academic arguments (and it seems most likely that it is by a Michelangelo follower in the sixteenth or seventeenth centuries), it is a fine piece of work, and the rather wooden poses of the supporting figures if anything reinforce the fluid movement of Christ's body between them.

It would be a pity to leave the Accademia without looking at the charming painting (Room 2) originally on the front panel of a cassone of the *Adimari Wedding* by an anonymous fifteenth-century master. In the background it is possible to make out the Baptistery, while underneath a coloured awning the guests arrive at the bride's house for a celebratory feast. Apart from giving an idea of dress and life in the fifteenth century among patrician families, and successfully evoking the atmosphere of an important occasion, it celebrates an event which for contemporary Florentines had much more than a simple Christian significance. Before this happy couple ever reached the altar their fathers would have spent months or years arguing over the exact financial details of what was, in effect, a political contract and business deal just as much as a religious event. Apart from involving large amounts of money (which was always of paramount importance in Renaissance society), marriage provided, as it still does, a precise fix on the social position and prestige of a Florentine family and it was taken, then as now, with deadly seriousness.

In the next room there is an early Botticelli and beyond in Room 3 a conventional Lorenzo di Credi (1459?–1537), a successful if predictable painter who, as though from a pattern book, rearranges a limited number of figures in different groups. He was a pupil of Verrocchio, taking over his studio in 1498. In the rooms to either side of the tribune containing the Michelangelo *David* there are some good pictures by important names such as Domenico Ghirlandaio and Pontormo, though perhaps the most enjoyable among them is by a less well known painter called Mariotto Albertinelli (1474–1515). In three rooms to the left of the tribune there is a collection of early Tuscan art.

*   *   *

Leaving the Accademia, turn left into Via Ricasoli and then left again into Via degli Alfani. At No. 78 is the **Opificio delle Pietre Dure**, a small but particularly agreeable gallery of inlaid *pietre dure*, those hard stones which are just slightly less precious than jewels—onyx, jade, lapis lazuli, malachite and so on. This is a craft unique to Florence which reached its zenith in the eighteenth century mainly because panels of inlaid *pietre dure*—which for obvious reasons tend to be very expensive—found a ready source of patronage from better off Grand Tourists. Looking at the objects in the ground-floor rooms, it is remarkable to observe how the texture and colour of different stones, when perfectly inlaid, can be used to achieve effects of depth and movement and can even, at its best, resemble landscape or portrait painting.

The most attractive of the medieval streets or borghi in Florence is the Borgo Pinti, at the far end of Via degli Alfani. Tall, narrow, highly picturesque but faintly claustrophobic, it runs all the way from the northern gates to the S. Croce quarter. Though it is still medieval in atmosphere, most of the palaces along its length were rebuilt surprisingly late, some of them in the seventeenth and eighteenth centuries. In the Palazzo Panciatichi Ximenes, immediately opposite at the crossroads, Napoleon spent most of June 1796.

About fifty yards to the north of where we stand is the church of **S. Maria Maddalena dei Pazzi**, perhaps the most lovely yet ironically one of least visited of the smaller churches in Florence (No. 58 on the right). Founded in the thirteenth century, added to in great style in the 1470s by Giuliano da Sangallo, and then completely redecorated at the end of the seventeenth century in honour of the Pazzi saint Maria Maddalena, it is an intriguing fusion of Renaissance austerity with baroque fantasy and exuberance. The measured, ordered discipline of the first courtyard, architecturally unusual for its square corner columns and strange capitals, contrasts with the interior of the church itself, a riot of colour with a *trompe l'oeil* ceiling by Jacopo Chiavistelli (1677) and a highly ornate marble chancel of roughly the same date enriched by the sculpture of Silvani and some hot baroque canvases by Luca Giordano.

A door to the right leads first to the Sacristy where there is some good rococo stucco-work, but more importantly to the crypt which contains one of the most compellingly moving works of art of the late fifteenth century in Italy. The route to the crypt, though a little tortuous, is wonderfully theatrical. A staircase leads down into the vaults, which are dimly lit and full of glass-fronted coffins in which you can just see bleached bones or a skull peeking out from musty ecclesiastic purple. Another staircase at the far side leads up into the crypt, which is usually empty but dominated by the *Crucifixion* (1493–6) on one wall, thought by many to be the masterpiece of Perugino (1446–1523) one of the greatest painters of his age, who was Raphael's first master.

Unlike the great majority of Perugino's art, which is exquisitely painted but perhaps emotionally rather vacuous, elegant but as cold as ice, the *Crucifixion* has a powerful sense of understated piety. The architecture itself forms the frame, and the triptych is divided on the lines of the ceiling vaults, so giving the impression that the landscape background is opening before us on to a green, perfectly still, rolling valley cut by a winding river, dotted with trees and hill-top towns. Christ and the saints to either side stand out in the foreground, almost as though the wall were made of glass and they were pushed against it. The impact of the painting derives from the curious gravity and obvious grief of the spectators who are arranged symmetrically to either side of Christ.

The Borgo Pinti leads south towards S. Croce. As it is perhaps not the safest street in Florence and reading a guide book while walking down it requires almost Michelangelesque feats of concentration and co-ordination, I will say nothing until you reach the end, where, if you cross the road and walk through the tunnel, you arrive in the enchanting little Piazza S. Pier Maggiore, which seems to combine all those people, sounds, and activities of a way of life that can have changed little over the centuries. There are beautiful gypsy girls running a market, butchers with blood-red cheeks and cherubic sons, a *latteria* selling wheels of Parmesan and goat's milk, a *polleria* where, if it is autumn, there will be pheasants, partridges and wild boar hanging by the door. The fruit market stands below what might be mistaken for the ruins of a Roman triumphal arch but is all that remains of the seventeenth-century church, destroyed in a fire in the 1770s, that gave the Piazza its name. That it was at one time an important and prosperous church is obvious from the engraving (40) (from Zocchi's *Vedute delle ville e d'altri luoghi della Toscana*, first published in 1744), made not long before it was destroyed by fire. Notice that the campanile in the background has now disappeared. The flat above the arches must surely be one of the most pleasant places to live in the city. We can only envy its occupant or the lucky individual who lives at the top of the Torre Donati, rising from the south side of the Piazza, which must enjoy one of the finest views of the Florentine panorama.

Continuing down Via Palmieri, take the second left into Via Ghibellina and continue for about 200 yards to the **Casa Buonarroti** (No. 70), also called the **Michelangelo Museum** (opening times, see p. 229).

Though called Michelangelo's house, he never lived here; its existence, however, is a monument to a side of his character sometimes forgotten — his pride in his semi-noble, if impoverished lineage and his overriding desire to restore his family to their former status. It was only in defiance of his family's wishes that Michelangelo

40

ever became an artist at all, and in old age he tried to make it clear that he had never been 'a painter or sculptor like those who set up shop'. He bought the site as soon as he had saved enough money, in 1508, and on his death in 1564 left it, with several of his works of art, to his nephew whose descendants lived here until they died out in the mid-nineteenth century. Though they presented their greatest pieces to the Medici in the sixteenth century—for instance the *Slaves* now in the Accademia—they retained some important early works, documents, letters and drawings and turned the house into a museum and shrine to Michelangelo's memory.

The most interesting rooms of the Casa Buonarroti are all on the first floor. In the room to the left of the landing is the *Battle Scene*, carved before 1492 while Michelangelo was only fifteen or sixteen, attached to the household of Lorenzo the Magnificent and studying sculpture under Bertoldo di Giovanni. Though clearly based on that sculptor's bronze *Battle Scene* now in the Bargello, this is the first example of Michelangelo's near obsession, obvious in his sculpture and his drawings, with writhing, interlocked male figures, and superbly accomplished for an artist still in his 'teens.

Opposite is Michelangelo's first known work, the *Madonna della Scala* (1490–1), a sweet Madonna and Child in low relief showing an obvious early influence from Donatello. In the room to the left is a model for his unexecuted façade of S. Lorenzo, which looks a little stark and charmless, though, enriched with sculpture as he intended, it would be more appealing. The Crucifix in the room to the other side of the landing was found in S. Spirito and attributed to Michelangelo in the early 1960s.

At the other end of the first floor are several rooms painted between 1613 and 1637 by the last generation of great Florentine painters as a celebration of Michelangelo's genius. The finest of them is the first, with windows giving on to Via Ghibellina, and paintings by most of the important seventeenth-century Florentine artists—including Cristofano Allori, Giovanni da S. Giovanni and Francesco Furini, though sadly not by the most famous among them, Carlo Dolci.

It is interesting, looking at their subject matter, to observe those episodes in Michelangelo's life on which artists of the seventeenth century chose to lay stress. Their interpretation of his character is very different from that generally held today, when we tend to think of him as the personification of the neurotic, difficult, quarrelsome artist, as a slave to his artistic personality, a creature of whim, or as a Bohemian who cared nothing for comfort. Here, however, he is presented as a man of distinction and importance—we see him being received by Doges, implored by Popes to finish the Sistine ceiling, and as an affable, polite, diplomatic courtesan.

The next rooms, which lead one from another further back into the house, are less important, but enjoyable, particularly the library by Cecco Bravo (a mid-seventeenth-century artist whose best work is seen at the Pitti), with a frieze of famous Florentines through the ages.

The room at the foot of the stairs is full of forgettable portraits of Michelangelo as an old man, mainly by artists who could never have seen him. In the rooms beyond there is an unusual little collection of paintings of the Buonarroti family that includes a fine Pieroesque panel by Giovanni di Francesco and a portrait attributed to Guido Reni.

From the Casa Buonarroti Via Ghibellina leads deeper into S. Croce. The third turning to the left (up Via de' Macci) will take you to the Mercato di S. Ambrogio, which is a little smaller but no less colourful than the Mercato Centrale at S. Lorenzo. To the north of the market is the church of S. Ambrogio, which you may still have time to visit before it closes at 12.45. In the chapel to the left of the high altar is a much admired tabernacle by Mino da Fiesole, made in 1481. If it is now closed you may like to avail yourself of the opportunity to try some of the small and reasonably inexpensive restaurants that surround the market. Otherwise you might return to Piazza S. Pier Maggiore, where you will find the trattoria Natalino (which is closed on Sundays); this is a cheerful restaurant though not among the cheaper ones. It is distinguished by having one wall elaborately frescoed by Pietro Annigoni, considered to be the most famous and possibly the most universally admired Florentine artist of the twentieth century. As you eat your meal here, you enjoy the bonus of taking in one of the 'sights' of Florence which many visitors may overlook.

10

THE FLORENTINE ENVIRONS

✤ Enlightened high-bourgeois Florentines of the Renaissance were the first Europeans to celebrate the pleasures of a rural existence, building villas near the city in which they could pursue their preferred rustic diversions. Fortunately few of their descendants share the same enthusiasm, displaying a healthy and entirely characteristic Italian antipathy to living anywhere but the city, with the happy result that most of the countryside around Florence remains delightfully unspoilt and that they still have some country left to dislike.

Though the plain of the Arno is now covered in dreary satellite towns, the hills that border on that plain are still relatively empty. To the south of Florence the country rolls to the edge of the city and it can be explored on foot. A ten-minute walk from the Ponte Vecchio will take you from the centre of the city to a landscape that for three hundred years foreign travellers have compared to a gigantic garden. The Costa S. Giorgio (see page 141), the most beautiful street in Florence, rises steeply from the Oltrarno to the Porta di S. Giorgio (c.1260), formerly twice its present height. Just beyond the gate is the entrance to the Forte del Belvedere, built between 1590 and 1595 on the orders of Grand Duke Ferdinando I to the designs of Buontalenti, which seems almost too elegant to be really menacing, as was its purpose. From here runs Via di S. Leonardo, an enchanting road that leads to **Arcetri**.

A few hundred metres along it, to the left, is the façade, much over-restored earlier this century, of the church of S. Leonardo. If open, it is worth venturing inside for it has a fine interior and contains a lovely thirteenth-century pulpit. Further on, a plaque marks the house rented by Tchaikovsky during the spring of 1878.

Via di S. Leonardo reaches and crosses Viale dei Colli then continues for a few hundred metres before it bends to the left and changes its name into Via V. Viviani and then left again to become **Via del Pian dei Giullari**. As the road steepens the view becomes progressively more entrancing and we pass (at No. 2) the Astrophysical Observatory of Arcetri with the first solar tower built in Europe (1872). Opposite is the Villa Capponi, with a justly famous garden that is sadly not open to the public. The enormous Torre del Gallo is a nineteenth-century reconstruction of a late medieval tower built and inhabited by Stefano Bardini (founder of the Bardini Museum) who lived in it for some of his life and used its enormous rooms to store some of the furniture and paintings he exported by the shipload to England and America. In the Villa La Gallina, which is beside it, are frescoes of nude dancers by that difficult and fascinating fifteenth-century artist Antonio del Pollaiuolo which visitors are sometimes shown by appointment. Galileo passed the final years of his life as a virtual prisoner at the Villa il Gioiello (No. 42) from 1631 until his death in 1642. The boredom of near house arrest was perhaps alleviated by a steady stream of distinguished visitors, including Thomas Hobbes and possibly Milton and, of course, the charm of the prospect from his *salotto*.

* * *

S. Domenico and Fiesole, to the north of Florence, are slightly further away and are reached by Bus no. 7 (from Via Cavour or Piazza S. Marco). Alight at **S. Domenico**, a collection of houses below Fiesole about three miles from Florence, in order to see the church of the same name. The church dates from 1406, though the present portico was added in 1612. Both the church and the adjoining convent are most interesting for their connection with Fra Angelico, as it was here that he lived from the late 1420s to the mid-1430s as a Dominican Observant before moving to the Friary of S. Marco. In the first chapel to the left is one of the most lovely examples of his early work—the *Madonna with Angels and Saints* of 1430 (light on right). The panels on the predella are copies, and the originals are in the National Gallery, London.

There are two good, if not wildly inspiring, late fifteenth-century paintings in the chapels off the right aisle: an interesting Botticellian painting (1st chapel), and a Lorenzo di Credi (2nd chapel). In the third chapel is an *Epiphany* by Jacopo da Empoli. It is worth ringing the bell at the Chapter House (No. 4) of the S. Domenico Convent, since it contains two frescoes by Fra Angelico—the *Crucifixion* (c.1430) and a detached fresco of the *Madonna and Child.*

Crossing the road and walking down Via delle Fontanelle, you will arrive at the Badia, a more important and much older church, which was once the Cathedral of Fiesole. The present façade is mid-twelfth century. It is less classically 'pure' than the roughly contemporary proto-Renaissance façades of S. Miniato and the Baptistery (the centre of the three arches is not semi-circular but a horseshoe, for instance) but no less interesting and looks particularly impressive since the rough stone surrounding the marble, added when the church was enlarged in 1464, emphasises the quality of the earlier encrustation. The Medici undertook the restoration and improvement of the Badia in the mid-fifteenth century, and it is from then that the present interior and the cloisters beside it date. Ask the sacristan for admission to the church.

We can now continue up to **Fiesole** either on foot or by the bus which grinds up a series of hairpin bends on the Via Fiesolana Nuova (built in the early nineteenth century). The more adventurous will choose to walk since the Via Fiesolana Vecchia, though not much less dangerous than the road to Bellosguardo, passes the lovely Villa Medici. This was probably designed by Michelozzo and built (1458–61) as a summer villa either by Cosimo il Vecchio or by his son Giuliano. The garden, raised up to the level of the ground-floor rooms, is the first in any Renaissance villa to be deliberately incorporated into the architecture. It is not open to the public but from the road you can smell the lemon trees, catch a glimpse of the garden and attempt to imagine the extraordinarily pleasant lives of those who have had the good fortune to live in it.

Climbing a little further up the hill, we arrive in the main Piazza of Fiesole. The cafés beneath the trees on the north side of the Piazza are a pleasant place to recuperate after our climb. Fiesole is only a little less famous than Florence. It was the preferred haunt of the foreign community who liked its view and also thought it cooler than Florence, which must in theory be true, though if it is now midsummer, we may find this difficult to believe.

The early history of Fiesole is not perfectly understood. It was probably occupied and fortified by the Etruscans, the pre-Roman Iron-age civilisation that dominated the larger part of the Italian peninsula from the fourth to the eighth centuries B.C., and it was certainly a thriving city under the Romans. Owing to its defensible position, Fiesole seems to have survived the ravages of the Dark Ages more successfully than Florence, and

hence its classical heritage is better preserved.

To the north of the Duomo is one of the best preserved Roman theatres in Tuscany. This is where a visit to Fiesole should begin. Built at the end of the first century B.C., the theatre was enlarged by Septimus Severus and Claudius and held an estimated three thousand spectators. To the right of the theatre are the Roman baths, probably built in the first century A.D. and enlarged by Hadrian. In front of them are three large rectangular swimming baths, the tepidarium, the frigidarium and the palestra. The small museum contains a collection of Etruscan and Roman urns and vases.

Little remains of late medieval Fiesole since the Florentines destroyed all of its buildings other than the Duomo after they conquered the city in the thirteenth century. The present over-restored façade of the Duomo looks uninviting but the interior comes as a pleasant surprise. The arrangement of choir over crypt is rather similar to that in S. Miniato. In the Salutati Chapel, to the right, are some of the best works of Mino da Fiesole, one of the greatest Renaissance sculptors, including his tomb of Bishop Leonardo Salutati (1465). The large altarpiece is by Bicci di Lorenzo.

The most attractive building in Fiesole is the Palazzo Pretorio, on the north side of the Piazza, with a loggia covered in the coats of arms of different podestà. Beside it the church of S. Maria Primerana was rebuilt between the sixteenth and seventeenth centuries. The interior has mid-trecento frescoes attributed to Taddeo Gaddi.

Fiesole's restaurants are dull, though it can be pleasant to sit out in the shade at either of the pizzerie in the Piazza. Those looking for a more ambitious fare are advised to walk to the Villa S. Michele, a fifteenth-century villa a little way below Fiesole on the new road, which is almost if not quite as beautiful as the Villa Medici and now a hotel, or take a taxi to *La Cisterna* in Maiano.

* * *

A little further from Florence (reached on buses 36 and 37 from the railway station) is the **Certosa del Galluzzo**, a fourteenth-century Cistercian monastery built mainly at the expense of Niccolò Acciaioli, a Florentine industrialist who seems to have intended that the building house not just a monastery but a school. Here I cannot resist the temptation to quote a passage from *Country Walks about Florence* of 1908 by Edward Hutton, a distinguished writer on Italy. It expresses attitudes commonplace among Anglo-Florentines at this date, but which today make one smile. After running through the history of the Certosa he allows himself to express a little personal opinion. 'Niccolò, however, died too soon to carry out his dream and at his death, the monastery being left without money, the school came to nothing and the library of precious manuscripts which he had founded there little by little was scattered again. And this might seem one of the greatest misfortunes, not for Florence alone but for all Italy, that when the monasteries were suppressed they were not put to the use of schools as they were in more than one case in England. A really great public school might have arisen on this hill in this Carthusian convent. An Italian Charterhouse, where carrying out the intention of the founder and generously expanding it, the Italian government, in our time at any rate, might have founded one of those splendid institutions which Italy so sadly needs.' This is perhaps not a point of view with which all will sympathise.

The Certosa is even more impressive within than without. A long staircase leads to a late sixteenth-century courtyard. Opening off it are the refectory, where we find Jacopo Pontormo's wonderful if badly deteriorated frescoes executed while he stayed here with his pupil Bronzino, avoiding the plague of 1522. The church, on the left side of the courtyard, is a good example of late sixteenth-century decoration and has fine frescoes over the altar by Poccetti, though its most celebrated treasure is the fifteenth-century tomb slab of Cardinal Acciaioli by Francesco da Sangallo. The essential reason for visiting the Certosa, however, still lies before us. It is to see and enjoy the Great Cloister, which is ringed by cells in which the monks pursued a life of prayer. Few places so powerfully evoke late medieval monastic life. About twenty of the 66 terracotta roundels in the cloister are thought to be the work of Giovanni della Robbia, the rest are by his workshop. Do not leave the cloister without a visit to one of the monastic cells, which, if not particu-larly luxurious or comfortable, have lovely views which must offer reasonable compensation for some of the more monotonous aspects of monastic life. Though not all monks and clerics lived so well, it is perhaps possible to understand why by about 1500 as many as a fifth of male Tuscans were attached in some way to the Church.

*   *   *

Florence looks its most lovely from **Bellosguardo**, just beyond the walls of the Oltrarno. Though only fifteen minutes on foot from Porta Romana or Piazza Torquato Tasso, only the bravest visitor will attempt the walk, bearing in mind the special contempt which Italian drivers reserve for the pedestrian, the steepness of the hill and the fact that the view in either direction as you climb is ingeniously obliterated by stone walls just higher than eye level. Wait for the last evening, hope that the weather is fine and take a taxi. The view is of a legendary beauty. If it is late evening in summer the sky will have a strange muddy phos-phorescence, the hills on the far side of the valley will be blurred into hazy silhouettes, fireflies will

dance among the olives and the vines that still run down to the walls. Beyond them, cut in two by a river, is a sea of red roofs surrounding Brunelleschi's dome that hangs on its white marble ribs. Seen in this light even the Pitti seems attractive. It is remarkable, if we look at the minutely detailed rendering of the same scene in 1863, by a protégé of Ruskin called John Brett, (41) to observe just how little it has changed over the last 125 years.

The Duomo, it is true, now has a new façade, the city walls are no longer complete, there are rather more houses on the slopes of Fiesole, but we have to look hard to find these differences. Florence is still, within and without, both amiable and unspoilt. With this scene firmly lodged in our minds we can now return to our hotel, pack our bags, pay the bill and reconcile ourselves to departure.

APPENDIX I

**Places of interest not mentioned in the text or
not normally open to the public, and some Medici Villas**

Not mentioned in text

Il **Museo di Firenze com'Era**, at Via del Oriuolo 24 (opening times, see p. 230) contains a collection of topographical material on the history of Florence. Of particular interest is its collection of old maps, plans and watercolours of the Mercato Vecchio.

The **Stibbert Museum** (Via Stibbert 26, north of the Piazza della Libertà) (opening times, see p. 231) was formed in the late nineteenth century by Frederick Stibbert, a self-made millionaire and compulsive collector. The collection is very large and wide-ranging, embracing things both incred-ibly dull and very exciting and beautifully arranged with a wild and occasionally romantic confusion that most will find charming. Stibbert's overriding interest was in arms and armour. This is brilliantly displayed and the only collection of its kind that I have ever seen and found interesting.

*   *   *

Not normally open to the public

The **Galleria Corsini** (entrance in Via Parione) is the largest and most impressive private gallery in Florence. It is generally shown to visitors at 12 o'clock on a Wednesday by a guide, but an appointment must be made by ringing 283044. With luck you will see the gallery on a sunny day since it has no electricity; though this endows the rooms with a unique charm, it can make it a little difficult to see the paintings if the weather is overcast.

Pause as you climb the great stone staircase from the courtyard to the Galleria to look at the seated statue (artist unknown) of the Corsini Pope Clement XII, who, when elected to office in 1730, was gout-ridden, decrepit and expected to live no more than a year. He surprised and irritated the College of Cardinals by surviving for a decade to impose his own highly reactionary will upon most aspects of Curial politics.

Double doors open into a vast ballroom with a painted ceiling representing the Palazzo's river façade as it was envisaged but never completed. Most of the doors around the room are false. When originally built and decorated the rooms probably had little more furniture than you see today. Their appearance was much changed, however, in 1945 since the eighteenth-century silk wall hangings, similar to those which can today still be seen in the Galleria Palatina at the Pitta, were so badly

cracked by vibrations from the blasts that destroyed the Ponte S. Trinita that they had to be taken down. The collection is particularly rich in the work of the now very fashionable central Italian painters of the seventeenth century. It includes a dozen or so paintings by Carlo Dolci, of which my own favourite is the *Muse of Poetry* beside the window on the right wall of the salone, the long room with windows giving on the river.

The most important paintings are in a small room at the far end of the salone; these include a late Botticelli and a Bellini.

The **Corridoio Vasariano** linking the Pitti and the Uffizi can be seen on a guided tour, places for which can be reserved at the ticket office of the Uffizi. The corridor covers about a quarter of a mile, and both its walls for almost the entire distance are covered in paintings. Many of these form an important collection of artists' self-portraits.

The **Cenacolo di San Salvi** (opening times, see p. 229) east of Florence and reached on Bus No. 10 from the station, No. 6 from Via Tornabuoni or on Bus No. 20 from the Piazza S. Marco, contains a famous *Last Supper* by Andrea del Sarto and paintings by Franciabigio, Ghirlandaio and others.

* * *

Some Medici Villas

The earliest Medici villas, such as **Caffagiolo** in the hilly area to the north of Florence called the Mugello, are better described as castellated farmhouses. It is from here that the obscure ancestors of the Medici migrated to seek and find their fortune in the thirteenth century. It is close to the road that leads north from Fiesole to Bologna over the Futa Pass, and can be reached by bus, though its interior is not open to the public. The present façades date from about 1450 when Cosimo I, eager to promote his own family history and to provide a suitable place to pursue his preferred rustic diversions, commissioned Michelozzo to enlarge and aggrandise what had been a modest-sized fortified house.

To the east of Florence towards Prato on the northern side of the Val d'Arno (Bus 14c) are the villas of **Carreggi**, famous for its connection with Lorenzo's Platonic Academy, and **Castello**, for which Botticelli painted the *Birth of Venus* and the *Primavera*. The Medici made a habit of dying at Carreggi and now the villa, appropriately, is a hospital. Their gardens are impressive despite the municipality's predilection for beds of marigolds. The view across the plain, which now embraces Scandicci and Sesto, some of the less romantic Florentine industrial suburbs, is less poetic that it must have once seemed. The interior of neither is open to the public.

La Petraia (Bus No. 28) only came into Medicean hands in the sixteenth century. The interior is open to the public. Unfortunately it took the fancy of Vittorio Emmanuele II who redecorated its rooms with a rich flamboyance which may not be to the taste of everyone who visits the villa today, but which all will admire as a fine period piece. The sitting room on the first floor looks like a saloon from a cowboy western set in the 1890s. The courtyard is enclosed by an iron and glass roof, which though doubtless more practical and convenient, has a disastrous effect on the general ambience. The frescoes around the walls by Volterrano and Giovanni da S. Giovanni are con-

sidered some of the most valuable examples of Florentine painting in the seventeenth century.

The most interesting and important of the Medici villas, however, is **Poggio a Caiano** which is about ten miles from Florence on the old Prato road. (42) (Take a COPIT bus No. 31 from the Piazza della Stazione. Both the garden and interior are open to the public; opening times, see p. 231.) It was designed by Giuliano da Sangallo, though he probably worked closely with his patron, Lorenzo the Magnificent. The villa was built in 1480–85. It is not large, yet it was conceived as more than a place for brief summer visits and it conforms perfectly with Alberti's description of the ideal country residence, which Lorenzo had certainly read. Both its exterior and interior are consciously architectural. Instead of the traditional open courtyard Sangallo built a large hall two stories high with a barrel-vaulted ceiling in gilded stucco. He cleverly adapts the antique villa to the requirements of Renaissance life, providing a balcony for the rooms on the piano nobile with the ground-floor arcades. The central loggia was added in the sixteenth century. The curving external staircase

is about a century later. Its most important interior decoration was commissioned not by Lorenzo but by his descendants. Sangallo's salone was frescoed at different times between 1512 and 1530 by Andrea del Sarto, Franciabigio, Pontormo (whose enchanting, summery, *Vertumnus and Pomona* of 1521 covers the right lunette) and completed by Alessandro Allori in the 1580s. Each scene glorifies the Medici by representing eminent members of the family as famous figures from Roman history. In the scene immediately to the left of the door, for instance, by Andrea del Sarto, Leo X is cast as Caesar. In the scene opposite by Allori, Lorenzo the Magnificent is represented as Scipio.

In the late seventeenth century it became the home of the Grand Prince Ferdinando de' Medici who used it as a gallery for his collection of Venetian art.

Through some accident of fate one of the greatest sixteenth-century Florentine paintings, Pontormo's *Visitation*, still hangs in the church of San Michele in the small town of **Carmignano**, about five kilometres from Poggio a Caiano (there is a local bus which connects the two towns). Seeing this unusually composed picture which has four figures, two of which stare at one another while the others gaze back at the spectator, then eating lunch in a café in Carmignano, is the perfect culmination to any morning. If, however, we have been sensible enough to hire a car we can continue on to the **Villa Artimino** which was built by Ferdinand I in 1590–94 to the designs of Buontalenti. Though it seems large enough to contain an entire court, it was intended only as a hunting lodge. The façade is more subtle in its appeal than it may at first seem. The loggia offsets the great expanses of white plastered wall around it while the buttresses create an effect of strength and simplicity and a cluster of chimneys sets off the long horizontals in the façade. The lovely staircase leading to the piano nobile was added in the last century on the basis of designs found in the Uffizi collection of drawings. The rooms on the Palazzo's piano nobile are open on Wednesdays.

The fattoria beside the villa has been converted into a small hotel with a good restaurant. This may be the perfect place to have lunch.

APPENDIX II

Opening times

Visitors to Florence have been known to express a certain indignation at the apparent illogicality of museum opening times which on occasion appear to have been deliberately designed to torment rather than oblige. Confusion results from the fact that State museums (that is, the largest and most important) close on Mondays, while those run by the City, the Church or other bodies do not. If not the simplest system, this at least ensures that there is something to see on a Monday. State museums also close on the main public holidays—1 January, Easter Day, 25 April, 1 May, first Sunday in June, 15 August, Christmas Day. Admission charges are now high, but on the first and third Saturday and the second and fourth Sunday of every month entrance to the State museums is free.

State museums close at two in the afternoon. None is open on Sunday afternoons. The Pitti perhaps presents the greatest challenge to the visitor attempting a rational use of time since all of its five museums are open simultaneously only on Tuesdays. Visitors should take care not to visit the Palazzo della Signoria on one of the many occasions when its energetic curators have decided to close down its most interesting rooms. If you find the Capella di Eleonora or the Studiolo di Francesco closed, ask for them to be opened.

Crowds in the Uffizi can be hard to avoid, though the gallery can empty out dramatically by late afternoon and feel half deserted by closing time. The Accademia is generally most crowded from 9 to 10.30.

Though churches display an admirable tolerance of the crowds that use them as galleries, they understandably discourage visits while a Mass is in progress. Generally they close their doors for two or three hours in the middle of the day, usually from 12.30. But smaller churches, for instance S. Maria Maddalena dei Pazzi, will probably not reopen until c.5 p.m. It is sensible to carry with you a supply of coins to turn on metered lights.

Following is a table of opening times for the principal museums and galleries. Please remember that these are liable to change.

Accademia, Galleria dell'
Via Ricasoli 60
    Weekdays ex. Monday, 9–2.
    Sunday and Holidays, 9–1.

Baptistery
Piazza S. Giovanni
    Daily, 9.30–12.30, 2.30–5.30.

Bardini, Museo
Piazza de'Mozzi 1
    Weekdays ex. Wednesday, 9–2.
    Sunday and Holidays, 8–1.

Bargello
Via del Proconsolo 4
    Weekdays ex. Monday, 9–2.
    Sunday and Holidays, 9–1.

Belvedere, Forte del
Via S. Leonardo
    Daily, 9–8.

Boboli Gardens
    Daily, 9 until dark.

Browning Museum (Casa Guidi)
Via Maggio
   Weekdays, 2–6.

Casa Buonarroti
Via Ghibellina 70
   Weekdays ex. Tuesday, 9–2.
   Sunday and Holidays, 9–1.

Cenacolo di San Salvi
Via Andrea del Sarto 16
   Daily ex. Monday, 10–1.
   Temporarily closed but visitable with an
   appointment made at Soprintendenza, Via
   della Ninna 5 (off Piazza della Signoria)

Certosa del Galluzzo
   Summer: Daily, 9–12, 4–7.
   Winter: Daily, 2.30–5. Can vary.

Chiostro dello Scalzo
Via Cavour 69
   Closed for restoration.
   Normally Daily, 9–1 ex. Monday.

Dante, Casa di
Via S. Margherita 1
   Weekdays ex. Wednesday, 9.30–12.30,
   3.30–5.30.
   Sunday and Holidays, 9.30–12.30.

Davanzati, Palazzo
Via Porta Rossa 13
   Weekdays ex. Monday, 9–2.
   Sunday and Holidays, 9–1.

Duomo
   Campanile and Cupola
      Daily, 8.30–12.30, 2.30–5.30.
      (Cupola shut Sunday)
   Museo dell' Opera
      Weekdays, 9.30–1, 2.30–5.30.
      Sunday and Holidays, 9–1.

Fiesole, Roman theatre
   Daily ex. Monday.
   Summer: 9–7.
   Winter: 10–4.

Firenze com' era, Museo di
Via dell' Oriuolo
    Weekdays ex. Thursday, 9–2.
    Sunday and Holidays, 9–1.

Horne, Museo della Fondazione
Via de' Benci 6
    Daily ex. Saturday, and every second Sunday,
    2–5.

Innocenti, Ospedale degli, gallery
Piazza SS. Annunziata
    Daily ex. Monday, 9–1.

Medici-Riccardi, Palazzo (Chapel)
Via Cavour 1
    Weekdays ex. Wednesday, 9–1, 3–5.
    Sunday and Holidays, 9–12.

Opificio delle Pietre Dure
Via degli Alfani 78
    Weekdays, 9–1.30.
    Sundays and Holidays, closed.

Pitti, Palazzo
    Palatine Gallery and State Apartments
        Weekdays ex. Monday, 9–2.
        Sunday and Holidays, 9–1.
    Museo degli Argenti
        Tuesday, Friday, 9–2; Sunday, 9–1.
    Gall. dell' Arte Moderna
        Weekdays ex. Monday, 9–2.
        Sunday and Holidays, 9–1.
    Porcelain Museum
    (Giardino del Cavaliere)
        Tuesday, Thursday, Saturday, 9–2.
    Clothes Museum
    (Palazzino della Meridiana)
        Tuesday, Thursday, Saturday, 9–2.
    Contini Bonacossi Collection
    (Palazzino della Meridiana)
        Tuesday, Thursday, Saturday, 9–2.
    (Appointment necessary)

Raccolta d'Arte Moderna Alberto Ragione
Piazza della Signoria
    Weekdays ex. Tuesday, 9–2.
    Sunday and Holidays, 9–1.

S. Croce
  Museo dell' Opera
    Daily ex. Wednesday, 9–12.30, 3–5.
    (6.30 in summer).
  Cloister and Pazzi Chapel
    Daily, 9–12.30, 3–5.
    (6.30 in summer).

S. Lorenzo
  Medici Chapels
    Daily ex. Monday, 9–2.
    Sunday and Holidays, 9–1.
  Laurentian Library
    Weekdays, 9–5. Sunday, closed.

S. Marco
  Weekdays ex. Monday, 9–2.
  Sunday and Holidays, 9–1.

S. Maria Novella, Chiostro Verde
  Weekdays ex. Friday, 9–7.
  Sunday and Holidays, 9–2.

Signoria, Palazzo della
  Weekdays ex. Saturday, 9–7.
  Sunday and Holidays, 8–1.

Stibbert, Museo
Via Stibbert
  Weekdays ex. Thursday, 9–2.
  Sunday and Holidays, 9–12.30.

Uffizi, Galleria degli
  Weekdays ex. Monday, 9–2.
  Sunday and Holidays, 9–1.

Medici Villas
  Poggio a Caiano
    Garden: Daily, 9 till dark.
    House: Public holidays (feriali) 9–1.30.
    Sunday and Festivals, 9–12.30.
  Villa della Petraia
    Weekdays ex. Monday, 9–2.
    Sunday and Holidays, 9–1.

INDEX

Accademia, 48, 202ff.
Agnolo, Baccio d', 124, 133
Albany, Louise, Countess of, 129
Alberti, Leon Battista, 80, 175, 189, 200, 225
Albertinelli, Mariotto, 206
Alfieri, Vittorio, 77, 129
Allori, Alessandro, 53, 82, 183, 201, 225
—, Cristofano, 162, 210
Ambrogio, S., 211
Ammanati, Bartolomeo, 48, 53, 61, 71, 126, 151, 195
Angelico, Fra, 93, 118ff., 214
Annigoni, Pietro, 211

Annunziata, SS., 195, 199ff.
Antella, Palazzo dell', 75
Antinori, Palazzo, 183
Apollonia, S., 117
Arcetri, 141, 148, 214
Aretino, Pietro, 157
—, Spinello, 147
Argenti, Museo degli, 169
Arno, River, 125ff., 137, 142
Artimino, Villa, 226

Baccani, Gaetano, 72
Bacciochi, Elisa, 20, 162, 164, 169
Badia, 73
— Fiesolana, 215

Baldovinetti, Alessio, 148, 199
Banco, Maso di, 82
—, Nanni di, 40
Bande Nere, Giovanni delle, 70, 109, 116
Bandinelli, Baccio, 48, 52, 71, 109, 202
Baptistery, 15, 25ff., 65
Bardi Chapels (S. Croce), 81
Bardini, Museo, 141
Bargello, 59ff.
Baroncelli Chapel (S. Croce), 82
Baroque art, 82, 108, 127, 132, 193, 198, 200, 207
Bartolini, Lorenzo, 80, 142

Bartolini, Lorenzo – *contd.*
—, Pensione, 127
Bartolini-Salimbeni, Palazzo, 124
Bartolomeo, Fra, 203
Beckford, William, 165
Bellini, Giovanni, 101, 222
Bellosguardo, 218ff.
Bellotto, Bernardo, 45
Belvedere, Forte del, 141, 151, 168, 213
Berenson, Bernard, 92, 131, 145, 199
Bertoldo, Giovanni di, 65
Biblioteca Nazionale, 126, 142, 165
Bicci di Lorenzo, 217
Blessington, Lady, 87, 113
Boboli Gardens, 151, 165ff.
Boccaccio, Giovanni, 73, 179
Borghese, Palazzo, 72
Borghini, Raffaello, 53
Botticelli, Sandro, 95ff., 193, 206, 222, 223
Botticini, Francesco, 134
Brancacci Chapel (S. Maria del Carmine), 130ff.
Bravo, Cecco, 211
Bronzino, Agnolo, 53, 54, 57, 100, 141, 202, 218

Browning, Robert & E.B., 91, 124ff., 135
Brunelleschi, Filippo,
    and Duomo cupola, 32, 35
    and S. Croce, 82ff.
    and S. Lorenzo, 110, 113
    and S. Maria Novella, 177, 180
    as architect, 133, 196
    as sculptor, 27, 40, 65
Bruni, Leonardo, 79
Buonarroti, Casa, 208ff.
Buondelmonte, Palazzo, 124
Buontalenti, Bernardo, 127, 179
    in the Uffizi, 98
    in the Pitti, 169, 171, 173
    as architect, 145, 191, 213, 226
Burckhardt, Jacob, 161
Byron, Lord, 100, 115, 129

Cafés and Restaurants:
    Angiolino, 193
    Cavallino, 57
    La Cisterna (Maiano), 217
    Il Fagiolo, 86
    La Loggia, 86
    La Maremma da Giuliano, 86
    Natale, 193
    Natalino, 212
    Omero, 148
    Pinchiorri, Enacoteca, 72
    Robiglio, 195
    Rivoire, 42, 87
    Sostanza, 193
    Vivoli, 74
Caffagiolo, Villa Medici, 223
Camaino, Tino di, 63
Cambio, Arnolfo di, 35, 63
Campanile, 28, 35
Canova, Antonio, 77, 156
Capponi, Gino, 77
Caravaggio, Michelangelo, 162
Carmignano, 225
Carmine, S. Maria del, 130ff.
Carrand, Louis, Collection, 67
Carreggi, Villa, 223
Casa Buonarroti, 208ff.
Casa Guidi, 135
Casentino, Jacopo del, 147
Castagno, Andrea del, 31, 61, 117, 201
Castellani Chapel (S. Croce), 82
Cathedral, 29ff., 195
Cavaliere, Giardino del, 168
Cellini, Benvenuto, 48, 49, 71, 202

Cenacolo di Fuligno, 116
— di S. Salvi, 222
Certosa del Galluzzo, 217
Chiavistelli, Jacopo, 207
Chiostro dello Scalzo, 121
Cioli, Valerio, 172
Cimabue, 83, 91
Cione, Nardo di, 179
Clark, Lord, 121
Clement VII, Pope (Giulio de'
    Medici), 18, 110, 112–13, 170
Cloisters: See under
    SS. Annunziata, Badia, Badia
    Fiesolana, Certosa del Galluzzo,
    S. Croce, S. Lorenzo,
    S. Maria Novella, Ognissanti,
    Chiostro dello Scalzo, S. Spirito
Clothes, Museum of, 170
Colonna, Agnolo, 171
Cooper, James Fenimore, 163
Cork, Earl of, 155
Corsini, S. Andrea, 132
—, Palazzo, 127, 221ff.
Cortona, Pietro da, 154, 161, 170
Cosimo, Piero di, 85, 198
Costa S. Giorgio, 141ff.,213
Crawford, Mabel, 168

Credi, Lorenzo di, 97, 206, 215
Croce, S. 74ff.
— Museum see Opera di S. Croce

Daddi, Bernardo, 42, 82, 85
Dante, Alighieri, 35, 67, 73, 77, 179
—, Casa di, 35
Danti, Vincenzo, 61
Davanzati, Palazzo, 186ff.
David (Donatello), 64
David (Michelangelo), 48, 203
Demidoff, Prince N., 142
Dolci, Carlo, 102, 160, 162, 222
Domenico, S. (Fiesole), 214
Domestic interiors, 85, 108, 186ff.
Donatello,
    in the cathedral buildings, 26, 28,
        33ff.
    in Or San Michele, 40ff.
    in the Bargello, 64ff.
    in S. Croce, 79, 82, 83
    in S. Lorenzo, 111
Dossi, Antonio, 84
Duccio di Buoninsegna, 91, 181
Dumas, Alexandre, 168
Duomo, 29ff., 195
—, (Fiesole), 216

Dürer, Albrecht, 101

Eliot, George, 141
Empoli, Jacopo da, 215

Fabbris, Emilio de', 202
Fabriano, Gentile da, 93, 108
Felicità, S., 139
Ferroni, Palazzo, 125, 127
Fiesole, 215ff.
— , Mino da, 69, 73, 211
Fiorentino, Rosso, 101, 111, 199
Firenze, Andrea da, 182
Firenze Com' Era, Museum, 221
— Nuovo, S., 73
Firidolfi, Palazzo, 135
Flood (1966), 76, 83, 125, 165
Foggini, G. B., 79, 132, 141, 200ff.
Forster, E. M., 74, 127, 196
Forte del Belvedere, 141, 151, 168,
    213
Foscolo, Ugo, 80
Fossombroni, Leonardo, 80
Fountains, 127, 151, 198
Francavilla, Pietro, 82,126
Francesca, Piero della, 94
Francesco, Giovanni di, 211

Franciabigio, 121, 199, 223, 225
Frescobaldi, Palazzo, 127
Fuligno, Cenacolo di, 116
Furini, Francesco, 73, 85, 210

Gaddi, Agnolo, 82, 147
—, Taddeo, 82, 83, 217
Gaetano, S., 183
Galileo, 79ff., 141, 156, 214
Gemito, Vincenzo, 63
Ghiberti, Lorenzo, 27ff., 40,41, 65, 181
Ghirlandaio, Domenico, 120, 206, 223
    School of, 36, 111
    in S. Maria Novella, 180ff.
    in S. Trinita, 191ff.
    in Ognissanti, 193
    in Osp. degli Innocenti, 198
Giambologna, 40, 42, 61, 173
    in Piazza and Palazzo Signoria, 48,49, 53
    in Bargello, 65, 72
    and SS. Annunziata, 198, 202
Giardino del Cavaliere, 168
Ginori, Palazzo, 117

Giordano, Luca, 108, 132, 207
Giorgio sulla Costa, S., 141
Giotto di Bondone, 67, 85, 91, 179
    the campanile, 28
    in S. Croce, 81
    in the Uffizi, 91
Giovanni, Giovanni da San, 170, 210, 223
Goes, Hugo van der, 97, 192
Goldoni, Carlo, 192
Gondi, Palazzo, 73
Gozzoli, Benozzo, 107ff.
Gray, Thomas, 153
Grazie, Ponte alle, 142
Grifoni, Palazzo, 196
Guadagni, Palazzo, 133
Guicciardini, Francesco, 136
Guidi, Casa, 135

Hawkwood, Sir J., 31
Hawthorne, Nathaniel, 181, 203
Hitler, Adolf, 87, 137
Horne, H. P., Collection, 85
Hugford, Ignazio, 95
Hunt, Holman, 166
Hutton, Edward, 41, 79, 217
Huxley, Aldous, 185

Innocenti, Ospedale degli, 196ff.

James, Henry, 28, 38, 158, 166

Lamberti, Niccolò, 41
Lanzi, Loggia dei, 46ff., 49
Laurentian Library, 112
Lawrence, D. H., 203
Leo X, Pope (Giovanni de' Medici), 18, 110, 114, 161
Leonardo (Arcetri), S., 214
Leonardo da Vinci, 51, 69, 97
Ligozzi, Iacopo, 202
Lippi, Filippino, 73, 95, 132, 134, 162, 181
—, Filippo, 94, 96, 111, 162
Loeser, Charles, Collection, 55
Loggia dei Lanzi, 46ff., 49
    — di S. Paolo, 183
    — of the Servites, 198
Lombardi, Francesco, 81
Lorenzaccio, 18, 71
Lorenzetti, Ambrogio, 93
—, Pietro, 85, 93
Lorenzo, S., 110ff.
Lorraine, Dukes of (1737–1859), 19, 151

Macchiaioli, The, 164
Machiavelli, Niccolò, 55, 79
Maiano, Benedetto da, 69, 79, 83,
    181, 185, 192
—, Giuliano da, 54
Majolica, 67
Manetti, Antonio, 148
—, Casa, 129
Mann, Sir Horace, 98, 129ff.
Mannerists, 101, 102, 111, 139, 151,
    199
Marco, S., 118ff.
Maria del Carmine, S., 130ff.
    — Maddalena dei Pazzi, S., 207
    — Novella, S., 175ff.
    — Primerana, S. (Fiesole), 217
Martini, Simone, 85, 93
Martino del Vescovo, S., 36
Masaccio, 31, 40, 93, 130ff., 177
Masolino, 93, 131
Medici, De' (family), 17ff., 105
    Alessandro (†1537), 18, 71
    Anna Maria (†1743), 19, 115, 151,
        153
    Cosimo il Vecchio (†1464), 17,
        106, 112, 118, 121
    Cosimo I (†1574), 46, 48ff., 88,

    101, 125, 151, 155, 158, 183,
        223
    Cosimo II (†1621), 19
    Cosimo III (†1723), 19, 116, 136,
        168, 169
    Ferdinando (†1713), 154, 156, 225
    Ferdinando I (†1609), 19, 198, 213,
        226
    Ferdinando II (†1670), 151, 157,
        170
    Ferdinando III (Grand Duke,
        1790–1824), 72, 163, 172
    Francesco (†1587), 51, 53, 127, 154
    Gian Gastone (†1737), 19, 80, 90,
        116, 149, 154, 155
    Giovanni di Averardo (†1429), 17,
        110
    Giuliano, Duke of Nemours
        (†1516), 114
    Leopold II (abdic. 1859), 20
    Lorenzo the Magnificent (†1492),
        17, 34, 106, 112, 170, 225
    Lorenzo, Duke of Urbino, 114
    Piero the Gouty (†1469), 147
    Pietro Leopoldo (Grand Duke
        1765–90), 20, 166, 170
Medici chapels, 113ff.

— tombs, 113ff.
—, Villa (Fiesole), 215
Medici-Riccardi, Palazzo, 105ff.
Mercato Centrale, 116
Mercato Vecchio (site), 36, 142
Michelangelo, 34, 77, 101, 126, 173
    in Piazza and Pal. della Signoria,
        46, 48, 51ff.
    in Bargello, 71
    in S. Lorenzo, 113ff.
    in Accademia, 202ff.
    Museum, 208ff.
Michele, Agostino, 171
    — Visdomini, S., 195
Michelozzo, 26, 106, 127, 147
    in S. Marco, 118
    in SS. Annunziata, 199, 200
    and Medici villas, 215, 223
Michelucci, Giovanni, 137
Miniato al Monte, S., 15, 146ff.
Mino da Fiesole, 216
Moderna, Galleria dell' Arte, 164ff.
Monaco, Lorenzo, 191
Montauto, Palazzo, 117
Mosaics, 26, 112, 146
Museo della Casa Antica Fiorentina,
    186ff.

Museo della Casa – *contd.*
— Nazionale *see* Bargello
Mussolini, Benito, 87

Napoleon Bonaparte, 100, 157, 206
Nardo di Cione, 179
Niccoli, Niccolò, 112
Niccolini Chapel (S. Croce), 82
— , Palazzo, 196
Niccolò sopr' Arno, S., 145
Nigetti, Matteo, 193

Ognissanti, 193
Opera del Duomo, Museo dell', 34ff.
Opera di S. Croce, Museo dell', 83
Opificio delle Pietre Dure, 206
Or San Michele, 38ff.
Orcagna, Andrea, 41, 74, 179
Origo, Iris, 166, 187
Ospedale di S. Giovanni, 193
— degli Innocenti, 196ff.

Panciatichi Ximenes, Palazzo, 206
Pancrazio, S., 190
Pandolfini, Palazzo, 121
Parigi, Alfonso, 169
Parmigianino, 102
Passignano, Domenico, 202

Pater, Walter, 63, 68, 69
Pazzi Chapel (S. Croce), 82ff.
— Conspiracy, 33
Perseus (Cellini), 49
Perugino, Pietro, 116, 202, 207
Peruzzi Chapel (S. Croce), 81
— , Piazza, 74
Petraia, Villa la, 164, 223
Pier Maggiore, S., 208
Pisano, Andrea, 27, 29
Pitti Palace, 149ff.
Pius IX, 116
Poccetti, Bernardino, 173, 192, 202, 218
Poggi, Giuseppe, 145
Poggio, Niccolò, 112
Poggio a Caiano, 225
Pollaiuolo, Antonio del, 70, 95, 214
— , Piero del, 95
Ponte alle Grazie, 142
— S. Trinita, 22, 126
— Vecchio, 22, 126, 137ff.
Pontormo, Jacopo, 139, 196, 225
in SS. Annunziata, 199, 202
in Accademia, 206
frescoes, 218
Pope-Hennessy, Sir John, 119

Porcelain, Museum of, 168
Pretorio, Palazzo (Fiesole), 217
Priors, 47, 55
Pucci, Palazzo, 195

Ragione, Alberto della, Collection, 57
Raphael, 46, 101, 121, 160
Reni, Guido, 158, 211
Repubblica, Piazza della, 22, 36ff.
Restaurants *see* Cafés
Ricasoli, Palazzo, 127, 192
Riccardi, Palazzo Medici-, 105ff.
Ricci, Stefano, 77
Ridolfi, Cosimo, 133
Robbia, Andrea della, 68, 196
— , Giovanni della, 68, 218
— , Luca della, 34, 39, 67, 83, 148, 192
Roman baths and theatre (Fiesole), 216
Romei, N., 193
Rosa, Salvator, 158
Rossellino, Antonio, 77, 148
— , Bernardo, 79, 201
Rossi, Vincenzo de', 52
Rossini, Gioacchino, 79

Rosso, Zanobi del, 73
Rubens, Peter Paul, 158, 159
Rucellai, Giovanni, 176, 190
—, Palazzo, 189
Ruggieri, Ferdinando, 73, 139
Ruskin, John, 33, 100, 149, 175
  on Giotto, 29, 91
  on Mino da Fiesole, 69
  on Orcagna, 74
  on Benozzo Gozzoli, 107
  on Andrea da Firenze, 182

Sabatelli, Luigi, 161
Salvi, Cenacolo di S., 222
Salviati, Cecchino, 54
Sangallo, Francesco da, 42, 70, 218
—, Giuliano da, 73, 134, 180, 185, 207, 225
Sarto, Andrea del, 223, 225
  in Chiostro dello Scalzo, 121
  in Pitti Palace, 158
  in SS. Annunziata, 199, 202
Sassetta, 145
Savonarola, Girolamo, 18, 55, 113, 121
Serristori-Cocchi, Palazzo, 75
  — (Demidoff), Palazzo, 145

Settignano, Desiderio da, 79, 192
Shelley, P. B., 90, 165
Signoria, Loggia della, 46
—, Palazzo della, 46, 50ff.
—, Piazza della, 45ff.
Silvani, Gherardo, 185, 207
Sloane, Sir Francis, 74
Spanish Chapel (S. Maria Novella), 182
Speccola, La, 136
Spirito, S., 110, 133ff.
Staël, Madame de, 77, 79
Stendhal, 129
Stibbert Museum, 221
Stockamer, Balthazar, 171
Strozzi Chapel (S. Maria Novella), 179, 180
—, Palazzo, 185
Summer Apartments (Pitti), 170
Sustermans, Justus, 159, 161, 164
Swinburne, A. C., 95, 135

Tacca, Pietro, 115, 198
Taddei, Palazzo, 117
Talenti, Simone, 39
Tchaikovsky, 214
Titian, 102, 111, 157, 158, 159

Torre della Castagna, 35
— del Gallo, 214
Tribunale della Mercanzia, 46
Trinita, S., 190ff.
—, Piazza S., 123ff.
—, Ponte S., 22, 126
Trollope, Anthony, 155
Trompe l'oeil, 130, 146, 171, 207
Twain, Mark, 155

Uccello, Paolo, 31, 93, 182
Uffizi, Palazzo & Gallery, 87ff.
Uguccioni, Palazzo, 46

Van Dyck, Sir Anthony, 158, 159
Vasari, Giorgio,
  as artist, 50ff., 77
  as architect, 88, 133, 139, 177
  as chronicler, 88, 92, 94, 106, 118, 201
Vasariano, Corridoio, 222
Vecchio, Palazzo, 46, 50ff.
—, Ponte, 22, 126, 137ff.
Veneziano, Domenico, 93
Venus (Canova), 156
Venus (Medici), 77, 98ff., 157
Verrocchio, Andrea del, 40, 69, 70,

Verrocchio, Andrea del – *contd.*
97, 110, 206
Vittorio Emmanuele II, 163, 164,
223
Victoria, Queen, 29
Villani, Giovanni, 16

Volterra, Daniele da, 72
Volterrano, Baldassare, 201, 223

Walpole, Horace, 129, 135, 153
Wilde, Oscar, 115
Winckelmann, 100

Wordsworth, William, 87, 139

Zocchi, Giuseppe, 127, 196
Zoffany, Johann, 98
Zoological Museum, 136
Zumbo, Gaetano, 136